MARCH
OF DEATH

THE NAPOLEONIC LIBRARY

Other books in the series include:

1815: THE RETURN OF NAPOLEON
Paul Britten Austin

ON THE FIELDS OF GLORY
The Battlefields of the 1815 Campaign
Andrew Uffindell and Michael Corum

LIFE IN NAPOLEON'S ARMY
The Memoirs of Captain Elzéar Blaze
Introduction by Philip Haythornthwaite

THE MEMOIRS OF BARON VON MÜFFLING
A Prussian Officer in the Napoleonic Wars
Baron von Müffling

WATERLOO LECTURES
A Study of the Campaign of 1815
Colonel Charles Chesney

WATERLOO LETTERS
A Collection of Accounts From Survivors of the
Campaign of 1815
Edited by Major-General H. T. Siborne

www.frontline-books.com/napoleoniclibrary

THE NAPOLEONIC LIBRARY

MARCH OF DEATH

SIR JOHN MOORE'S RETREAT TO CORUNNA, 1808–1809

Christopher Summerville

'The horrors of this retreat have been again and again described in terms calculated to freeze the blood of such as read them; but I have no hesitation in saying that the most harrowing accounts which have yet been laid before the public, fall short of the reality.'
General Charles Stewart, 3rd Marquess of Londonderry

Frontline Books

This book is humbly dedicated to
Ewa Haren and Paula Czaczkowska

March of Death

A Greenhill Book

First published in 2003 by Greenhill Books, Lionel Leventhal Limited
www.greenhillbooks.com

This edition published in 2015 by

Frontline Books
an imprint of Pen & Sword Books Ltd,
47 Church Street, Barnsley, S. Yorkshire, S70 2AS
For more information on our books, please visit
www.frontline-books.com, email info@frontline-books.com
or write to us at the above address.

ISBN: 978-1-84832-830-3

CIP data records for this title are available from the British Library

Designed and Edited by Donald Sommerville
Printed and bound by CPI Group (UK) Ltd, Croydon, CR0 4YY

Contents

List of Maps

List of Illustrations

Introduction

Sir John Moore's winter campaign of 1808–09 has become the stuff of legend. A small British army, sent to help Spain rid herself of Napoleon's invading legions, strikes a last-minute blow in the cause of freedom, before being forced to retire in the face of overwhelming numbers. Abandoned by their Spanish allies, and chased at the sword's point by the Emperor himself, a headlong flight over the Cantabrian Mountains ensues, culminating at the port of Corunna, where, with no ships to save them, the redcoats are obliged to make a final stand. It is a story which scintillates with excitement, drama, endurance, and heroism. It is also a story darkened by despair, appalling suffering, tarnished honour, and betrayal.

The tale is also one which is peopled by a cast of larger-than-life personalities: Napoleon, willing to sacrifice an army to smash the British; Marshal Soult, the 'Duke of Damnation', obliged to learn respect for his enemy; and Sir John Moore, sent on an impossible mission by London and as a consequence, expected to save the British army single-handed.

There have been several accounts of the Corunna Campaign over the years, most of them contained within biographies of Moore, its enigmatic hero. Why then, the need for another? My aim in writing this book was threefold: firstly, to squeeze Moore back onto bookshelves burdened with volumes on Napoleon and Wellington; secondly, to present –

Introduction

as far as possible – a strictly chronological account of the Corunna Campaign; and thirdly, to pick up the gauntlet thrown down by General Charles Stewart, 3rd Marquess of Londonderry, over 160 years ago, when he wrote,

> 'The horrors of this retreat have been again and again described in terms calculated to freeze the blood of such as read them; but I have no hesitation in saying that the most harrowing accounts which have yet been laid before the public, fall short of the reality.'

In order to pack as much narrative power as possible, I have relieved heavily on the testimonies of those who were there – diaries, journals, and memoirs long out of print. I have, however, in the interests of clarity and consistency, seen fit to take the occasional liberty with this material: standardising spellings, and revising punctuation for the benefit of the modern reader. I hope the purists will forgive me.

Sources, where definitely known, are given in the notes at the end of each chapter or listed in the bibliography. As for Moore's words, they were mainly culled from the correspondence and official documents contained in his brother James' book, *Narrative of the Campaign of the British Army in Spain, Commanded by His Excellency, Lieutenant-General Sir John Moore, K.B.* However, a few choice lines were taken from, Major-General Sir J. F. Maurice's, *The Diary of Sir John Moore*; and also from the file 'Documents Relating to Sir John Moore', lodged in the Public Record Office.

For the reader's convenience, I have included maps showing the Iberian Peninsula in 1808–09, the route taken by the British on their retreat to the coast, and the dispositions of Moore's and Soult's forces at the Battle of Corunna.

Moore's order of battle, the losses sustained by his army during the campaign, and brief biographical notes on some of the book's major sources, may be found in the appendices.

Finally, I would like to thank the following people for their invaluable help and support: Laurence Cornhill, Paula Czaczkowska, Andy Dove, Paul Doughty, Brent Fiddeman,

Introduction

Ewa Haren, Captain D. D. Horn, Dr Martin Howard, Jonathan North, Gervase Phinn, Steve Powell, Andrew Tarring, Ralph Thompson, Colin Worley.

Christopher Summerville,
York 2003

Prologue

'They are a nation of shopkeepers, their glory is in their wealth.' In this famous Napoleonic jibe at the British may be found the origin of the conflict in the Iberian Peninsula, for it was economic war with Britain which sparked Napoleon's interest in the affairs of Portugal and Spain, leading him into a war which would last almost seven years, from 1807 into 1814, and which he would come to call his 'Spanish ulcer'.

In July 1807 Napoleon was at the pinnacle of power. The Treaty of Tilsit had brought to a successful conclusion his war of conquest in central and eastern Europe, and he found himself the Emperor of Europe – a latter-day Charlemagne – with the power to create and dismember kingdoms at will. The 'nation of shopkeepers', however, remained defiant, and Napoleon knew that, in order to feel secure in his power, that defiance must be broken.

Apparently safe behind the wooden walls of her navy, Britain was, in fact, isolated and potentially vulnerable. Trade was her lifeblood and Napoleon – who had managed to constrict its course the previous year, with the introduction of an economic blockade known as the Continental System – now sought to stem the flow entirely. The logical continuation of the Continental System envisaged a total ban on British goods throughout Europe. Napoleon hoped that by closing Continental ports to British merchantmen, he could starve

'Perfidious Albion' of cash, and as a consequence, bring her to heel. The plan would only work, however, if the entire coastline of Europe could be hermetically sealed off from British shipping, and therein lay the root of Napoleon's disastrous post-Tilsit foreign policy: for Britain was the workshop of the world and everyone – including the French – wanted British wares.

Unchallengeable mistress of the seas since the victory at Trafalgar in 1805, Britain retaliated with a maritime blockade of her own, seizing any vessel bound for French ports and imposing heavy fines on those wishing to do business with the Emperor. This move escalated the economic conflict, provoking a predictable response from Napoleon: 'The English say they will not respect neutrals at sea; I will not recognise them on land.' And so, as the two great powers locked horns over lucrative markets, non-aligned nations became caught in the crossfire.

Portugal for instance, relied heavily upon healthy trade links with London and considered herself 'England's oldest ally'. Consequently, when Napoleon began bullying Prince John of Braganza to close his ports to British ships, the Portuguese Regent was reluctant to comply. A flurry of French ultimata followed and John, seeking to soothe the Emperor's wrath, eventually made several half-hearted concessions; but Napoleon was not impressed and promptly sent 24,000 troops under General Andoche Junot into Spain – a nominal French ally – with orders to march on Lisbon.

With Spanish collusion, Junot entered Portugal and, facing little organised resistance, occupied the capital on 30 November 1807. Thanks to the British Royal Navy, however, Prince John and the Portuguese royal family, the bulk of their considerable treasure, and the Portuguese fleet had disappeared over the oceanic horizon *en route* for Brazil. Denied these prizes, Junot could, nevertheless, congratulate himself on achieving his primary object, for, despite some pockets of unrest, Portugal seemed set to become yet another French satellite.

But, for Napoleon, Junot's success was merely the first phase in a plan to put the whole peninsula in his pocket: 'Convinced as I am that I shall never secure lasting peace with England until I set the whole of Europe in motion', he explained to his brother Louis, 'I have determined to put a French prince on the throne of Spain.' From the Emperor's point of view, Spain was ripe for takeover, mismanaged as it was by a corrupt, inefficient, and unpopular régime – a rotten door which, with a single kick, might be removed for the good of all. The final phase of his plan, then, was the subjugation of his unsuspecting ally – and another nail in the coffin of British commerce.

In 1807 Spain was one of the most backward nations of Europe, its landscape wild and untamed, its infrastructure underdeveloped, and its people impoverished. The country's affairs were controlled by an unspeakable quartet: the elderly and imbecilic King Carlos IV; his domineering and adulterous wife, Queen Maria Luisa; their treacherous son Ferdinand; and Maria's lover, the immoral and generally loathed Prime Minister, Manuel Godoy. Together they formed a bickering, dysfunctional family, in which only Ferdinand, Prince of the Asturias, enjoyed any popular support, and only Godoy any real executive power.

An ally of France since 1796, Godoy's enthusiasm for Napoleon's cause had cooled considerably since his country's catastrophic defeat at Trafalgar, where, at the hands of Horatio Nelson, the bulk of the Spanish fleet had been annihilated. Indeed, within twelve months of that debacle, Godoy was making overtures to Napoleon's enemies with a view to swapping sides at the first opportunity. Napoleon, however, did not miss a trick, and when he determined to annex Spain, the venture had the added appeal of punishing a treacherous ally.

Napoleon resorted to guile to achieve his goal of undermining Godoy's position. Under the pretext of reinforcing Junot's army in Portugal, he flooded Spain with troops. On 16 February 1808 they took control of the

Pyrenean passes and the Spanish border forts, and on 24 March Marshal Murat – Napoleon's brother-in-law and acting commander-in-chief in Spain – entered Madrid with 118,000 men. At first, the French were welcomed as friends and allies, liberators even, from the despotic rule of the hated Godoy. As Napoleon had calculated, the influx of foreign troops quickly destabilised Spain's political situation, and popular protests broke out in support of Ferdinand. In fact, King Carlos and his Queen (with Godoy's connivance) had already attempted to flee the country, only to be thwarted by an angry mob, which demanded Godoy's dismissal and the King's abdication in favour of his son.

It was at this point that Napoleon personally intervened, inviting the Spanish royal family to France, where, with himself as mediator, Spain's deepening crisis might be settled amicably. Suspecting nothing, the royals agreed and walked straight into Napoleon's trap. Within weeks, Carlos, Maria and Ferdinand were languishing in exile, having been coerced into renouncing their hereditary claims to the throne. As for Godoy – who had been found by French troops following his fall from grace, hiding from the mob under a pile of mats in the rafters of his mansion – he followed Carlos and Maria into exile at Compiègne. This left Napoleon free to arrange for pro-French factions in Madrid to 'request' that his brother, Joseph Bonaparte, be 'elected' king. Thus, by 6 June 1808, the Emperor's plan appeared to have succeeded perfectly.

But Napoleon had not counted on the reaction of the Spanish people. Following the disappearance of their royal family, the Spaniards had become restive, and on 2 May, at Madrid, anti-French riots broke out. Murat brutally suppressed this outburst and tensions were still running high when the news of Joseph's accession pushed the populace into a general insurrection, in which Ferdinand was pronounced a martyr, and 'war to the knife' was declared upon the French.

Despite the storm of patriotic fervour, however, there was little concerted action. Militant local governments or *juntas* sprang up in the provinces, but they rarely worked in harmony, agreeing on nothing but the obvious need to eject the French. As for the Spanish regular army, years of neglect, mismanagement and personal rivalries among its top brass, had reduced it to a rabble, lacking weapons, uniforms, transport and even horses for the cavalry. Nevertheless, the country was aflame with hatred for the French, and the passion of the Spanish patriots was blessed with a garland of early victories. The most notable of these occurred on 19 July at Baylen, a town in the southern province of Andalusia, when General Dupont was defeated and his entire corps of almost 18,000 men captured. This event sent shockwaves around the world, destroying the myth of French military superiority, and replacing it with the illusion of Spanish invincibility.

On hearing of these reverses, Joseph – the 'Intrusive King' – who had entered his new capital on 22 July, promptly fled back behind the River Ebro, within reach of the Pyrenean passes, taking 20,000 French soldiers with him. The Spaniards were ecstatic and considered the war as good as won. Basking in a wave of euphoria, they formed a Supreme *Junta*, in order to fill the power vacuum left at Madrid; but instead of capitalising on recent successes, this body frittered away the initiative in a round of backslapping, spending its days voting honorary distinctions and liberal salaries upon its own members.

Meanwhile, news of the catastrophe at Baylen – and Joseph's ensuing flight – reduced Napoleon to tears of rage. Realising that, 'the harm done is nothing to the dishonour', he determined to set matters right, so while the 'highnesses' and 'excellencies' of the Supreme *Junta* relaxed, Napoleon prepared to march on Madrid at the head of an army of 80,000 veterans.

Nowhere was the news of Spanish successes more welcome than in London, where, augmented by sweltering temperatures of over 98° F (37° C), a kind of 'Spanish fever' had taken hold. Past enmities were forgotten, as British society went mad with fabulous notions of Hispanic heroism and zeal. The press launched a popular campaign in support of the rebels, referring to Britain's erstwhile foe as 'a brave and noble nation', while contemporary poet Tom Campbell gushed, 'Oh sweet and romantic Spain! If the Spanish plume and beaver succeed I shall die of joy – if not, of grief.' British enthusiasm turned to delirium, however, when deputies from the Supreme *Junta* arrived in London seeking aid, and as Arthur Bryant notes in his book, *Years of Victory*, 'For a moment the whole nation was united.'

And indeed it was, for even the politicians, irrespective of party loyalties, were unanimous in their support for the Spanish insurrection. As for the Tory Government – under the nominal leadership of the ageing and infirm William Bentinck, 3rd Duke of Portland – it was dominated by two powerful pro-Spanish figures: the Foreign Secretary, George Canning, and the Secretary for War, Robert Stewart, Viscount Castlereagh. Both fervently backed the Spanish cause, and both were looking for an excuse to send British troops into action on the European mainland. The Spanish deputies, however, were insistent that they did not want direct military intervention; they had simply come to ask for cash. And they got it – £1.5 million in silver (over £60 million by modern reckoning) – as well as 120,000 muskets, millions of cartridges, 155 artillery pieces, 100,000 uniforms, and an assorted glut of other military supplies. Meanwhile, diplomatic relations with the *Junta* were cemented with the appointment of John Hookham Frere (a long-time friend of Canning's) as British envoy at Madrid.

The question of British military involvement, however, would not go away; the politicians wanted it, the press wanted it, the people wanted it. Only the Spaniards – mistrustful of London's motives – remained lukewarm. And yet they continued to agitate the martial spirit of their newfound friends with hints of further glory to come. Eventually, the pressure to act could no longer be stemmed and, on the advice of the Spanish diplomats, it was decided to mount an expedition to Portugal, in order to evict the stranded soldiers of General Junot. The success of the enterprise was assured, London believed, since its forces would be acting in concert with vast Spanish armies, which, in their turn, would be supported by an implacable nation in arms. However, as the contemporary historian and Peninsular War veteran, Sir William Napier, points out:

> 'Nothing could be more unsound, more eminently fallacious, than the generally entertained opinion of French weakness and Spanish strength ...At a distance, the insurrection appeared of towering proportions and mighty strength, when in truth it was a fantastic object, stained with blood and tottering from weakness.'

No Such Command
Since Marlborough

Castlereagh eventually cobbled together 40,000 troops for his Peninsula crusade, culled from contingents in Ireland, England, and Gibraltar. By mid-July, he had already sent the first of these parties to Portugal, under the command of Lieutenant-General Sir Arthur Wellesley, who had returned from India a few years before with a string of spectacular victories to his name. Wellesley – who would later find fame as the 1st Duke of Wellington – landed at Mondego Bay on 1 August with 13,500 troops and instructions from Castlereagh to give 'the Spanish and Portuguese nations every possible aid in throwing off the yoke of France.' This he proceeded to do, thrashing Junot three weeks later at the Battle of Vimiero, fifty miles north of Lisbon. Left to his own devices, Wellesley might have crushed the French single-handed, but it was not to be, for Castlereagh had appointed two senior generals to oversee the campaign, and when they arrived, Wellesley was superseded.

First on the scene was fifty-three year-old Lieutenant-General Sir Harry Burrard,[1] favourite *aide-de-camp* of the Duke of York, who arrived at the height of Wellesley's battle. He graciously refrained from interfering with his junior's plans until victory was assured, when he called an immediate ceasefire. Wellesley eagerly pointed out that Junot's line of retreat was begging to be cut, and that by committing fresh troops, Burrard might win not only the battle, but also the war. Burrard, refused to listen, however, and the French were suffered to escape. Next day, fifty-eight year-old General Sir Hew Dalrymple[2] made his appearance. Dalrymple had spent the previous two years as Governor of Gibraltar and was more of a diplomat than a warrior; indeed, despite his rank, he had never commanded an army in the field. Now he assumed the command-in-chief, with Burrard as his second. His first act was to congratulate Burrard on his caution; his second was to call an armistice, and enter into peace negotiations with Junot. Thus, while British reinforcements were landing up the coast at Mondego Bay, Dalrymple and Burrard concluded a convention with the French, whereby they would quit Portugal in return for a safe passage home in British ships, together with weapons, colours, and accumulated Portuguese plunder. The deal was done at Dalrymple's headquarters at Cintra, close to Lisbon, and instantly caused a storm of controversy in both Portugal (where people felt themselves betrayed) and in Britain (where people felt themselves dishonoured). In London, the popular press pilloried the British generals, printing the text of the Cintra treaty surrounded by heavy, black funereal borders. Lord Byron, the poet, was particularly appalled, and set about attacking 'Betty' Burrard and 'Dowager' Dalrymple in verse:

> Here folly dash'd to earth the victor's plume,
> For chiefs like ours in vain may laurels bloom.

The upshot of the Convention of Cintra[3] – apart from the bloodless liberation of Portugal – was a court of inquiry, launched in London, where Dalrymple, Burrard, and the unfortunate Wellesley (who was also a signatory) were summoned to explain their actions. Meanwhile – despite Dalrymple's unspectacular methods – it had to be admitted that the primary objective of the expedition, namely, the expulsion of Junot from Portugal, had been achieved. The British, however, were still consumed by 'Spanish fever', and

Castlereagh decided to send the army – languishing at Lisbon since Vimiero – across the border to bolster the much-vaunted insurrection there. With three top generals gone in a flash of public indignation, however, who was to head this new initiative? Much to Castlereagh's embarrassment, there was only one option: Lieutenant-General Sir John Moore, the one man he had done everything in his power to thwart.

> 'Tall and extremely good-looking, strong and upright
> ...He was known to be heroically brave, wholly
> uncorrupted and incorruptible ...There was something
> god-like about him.'

Sir John Moore, described above by Christopher Hibbert in his book *Corunna*, was Britain's foremost soldier and as such, the obvious candidate for command. Born in Glasgow, Scotland, in 1761, Moore – the son of a local physician – had entered the army as an ensign at the tender age of fifteen. Since then, he had seen service as a regimental infantry officer in North America, the West Indies, Ireland, the Netherlands, and Egypt. In 1803 he had taken command of a brigade at Shorncliffe, deployed for home defence. Here he had made his name as an innovative instructor, pioneering and developing light infantry tactics, thus creating the first corps of modern soldiers in the British Army. He was rewarded for his services with a knighthood, promotion to the rank of lieutenant-general, and a string of independent commands in Sicily, Gibraltar, and Sweden.

Moore's credentials for command extended far beyond mere military experience, however, for the man oozed charisma: his speech was simple and direct; his reports witty and precise; his devotion to duty and his desire to set any wrong to right, passionate. He was a humanitarian, who abhorred the use of the lash (declaring on one occasion, that it would be unfair to flog soldiers for drunkenness, unless officers were flogged for it too!), and insisted that soldiers be treated with kindness and respect. In short, Moore set himself high standards in everything he undertook, and expected others to follow this lead. A consummate soldier, he had remained single – despite a legion of female admirers – considering himself wedded to his profession.

He was, however, unpopular with the Portland ministry, which he frequently embarrassed with cogent, commonsensical criticisms on matters of policy. An ex-Member of Parliament himself, Moore was not afraid to take ministers to task, especially when they found themselves floundering in the military sphere. His particular targets, therefore, were Secretary for War Lord Castlereagh, and Foreign Secretary George Canning, for whom he had become something of a *bête noir*. Sadly for Sir John, he had selected for his victims perhaps the two most powerful men in the country. Relations between Moore and his political masters had been further soured by a recent sojourn in Sweden. Sent to the aid of King Gustavus IV – whose country was menaced by the armies of France, Russia, and Denmark – Sir John was promptly arrested by the mad king for daring to offer advice, and forced to flee the country disguised as a peasant. Botched, embarrassing missions aside, Moore was also an ideological opponent of the government, consistently exhibiting liberal tendencies which conservative ministers viewed with suspicion. Consequently, despite obvious talent and experience, Moore had been deliberately overlooked at the outset of the Peninsula campaign, in favour of those more politically correct.

But with the recall of Dalrymple and Burrard, Moore was technically next in line for command, and the government had little choice but to call upon his services. For Castlereagh and Canning, however, this mortifying little cloud had a silver lining: if Moore succeeded, then they could legitimately claim the credit for having appointed him; if he failed, however, they could sidestep any unpleasant consequences, by blaming a priggish *prima donna* they privately loathed.

Thus it was, that on 6 October 1808, at his headquarters in Lisbon, Lieutenant-General Sir John Moore received the following despatch from London:

> 'His Majesty having determined to employ a corps of
> his troops of not less than 30,000 infantry and 5,000

cavalry in the north of Spain, to co-operate with the Spanish armies in the expulsion of the French from that kingdom, has been graciously pleased to entrust to you the command in chief of His forces.'[4]

Moore had sailed to Portugal as Burrard's understudy, and this low-profile role had saved him from the furore surrounding Cintra. Consequently, he read the above message with a mixture of satisfaction and bemusement. Satisfaction because, as he himself noted, there had been 'no such command since Marlborough for a British officer'. Bemusement because he knew full well that the British government had done everything in its power to keep him from command:

'How they came to pitch upon me I cannot say, for they have given sufficient proof of not being partial to me.'

Indeed they had not. And it has been suggested by some of Moore's supporters that, in placing him under the orders of two virtually unknown – albeit senior – generals, Castlereagh was casting a deliberate slight, in the hope of securing his resignation. Sir John was certainly mortified at the government's 'unhandsome' treatment of him, and parted from Castlereagh on frosty terms, prophesying failure for the expedition. Now, much to the surprise of all concerned, he found himself at the head of the army after all, charged with the task of leading it into Spain. But what was he to do when he got there? No one – including Castlereagh – seemed sure, for apart from the directive to 'co-operate with the Spanish armies,' Moore's only other guideline from London was to:

'...take the necessary measures for opening a communication with the Spanish authorities for the purposes of framing the plan of the campaign, on which it may be advisable that the respective armies should act in concert.'

These words were dismissed by Moore as 'a sort of gibberish.'

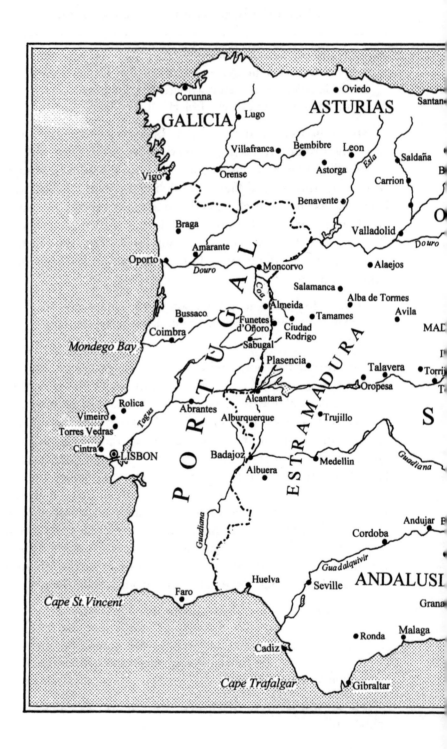

FRANCE

San Sebastian
Bayonne
Bilbao
Tolosa
THE PYRENEES
Vitoria
Pampeluna
NAVARRA
Figuras
Rosas
Logrona
Tudela
Ebro
Gerona
STILE
Saragossa
Lerida
CATALONIA
Calatayud
Belchite
Barcelona
Alcaniz
Tarragona
Tortosa
Tagus
BALEARIC ISLES
Cuenca
MINORCA
EW CASTILE
MAJORCA
I N
Valencia
MURCIA
MEDITERRANEAN SEA
Alicante
Murcia
Cartagena

ARAGON
VALENCIA

0   50   100
MILES

Chapter 1

With 10,000 men required for the defence of Portugal, Moore's immediate command consisted of some 20,000 troops, available for operations over the Spanish frontier. They were to be augmented by a further 12,000 men under Sir David Baird, already on their way from England. It was a largely inexperienced army – some regiments had not seen service since the Seven Years' War of 1756–63 – and most soldiers were unused to the rigours of campaign life. They were all, however, volunteers: some serving for adventure, some from a genuine sense of patriotism, others to avoid a prison sentence. The average age of the soldiers was twenty-three, and their average height 5 feet 6 inches. Most had been farm labourers, many from impoverished villages in Ireland or Scotland. They were paid one shilling per day, and led by an officer corps of aristocrats and gentlemen, many of whom had simply bought their commissions and had never received any formal military training. All were eager for action, however, and glad to be under the command of Moore, whose reputation was such, that they believed him to be invincible.

Moore saw the need to get moving as soon as possible, before autumnal rains turned the roads to mush, making a swift rendezvous with Spanish forces unlikely. But how best to move his men quickly from the west coast of Portugal to the heart of Spain? Two possibilities presented themselves: a sea-voyage to Corunna, on the north-western tip of Spain, followed by a hike inland; or an overland trek across Portugal, over the border, and into the heart of Spain. Sir John dismissed the former option, considering a seaborne passage to be risky, and believing (correctly, as it turned out) that Corunna would be unable to support both his own army and that of Sir David Baird, *en route* to the port from Falmouth. Having settled on the second option, however, Moore was perplexed by the fact that no one – including the Portuguese – seemed to have any reliable knowledge as to the state of the roads leading into Spain. Furthermore, it appeared that the army possessed inadequate transport for the carriage of ammunition and stores. Neither could he buy or hire enough carts for the purpose, his measly military chest of £25,000 being totally insufficient. Meanwhile, the Lisbon merchant supposedly supplying the needs of the British had rather inconsiderately gone bankrupt. Thus, on 9 October, Moore was moved to complain to Castlereagh:

> '...the army is without equipment of any kind, either for the carriage of the light baggage of regiments, artillery stores, Commissariat stores, or other appendages of an army; and not a magazine is formed in any of the routes by which we are to march.'

As for the soldiers – the victors of Vimiero – two months of idleness had softened them up, and an alarming number were reporting themselves sick. Moore, however, simply blamed the soldiers' lust for alcohol, and issued the following reprimand:

> 'The General assures the troops, that it is owing to their own intemperance, that so many of them are rendered incapable of marching against the enemy: and having stated this, he feels confident that he need say no more to British soldiers to insure their sobriety.'

These were words which, considering the disgraces which lay ahead, were laden with irony.

Meanwhile, preparations for the march went ahead, and Sir John, in an effort to circumvent the transport crisis, ordered all heavy baggage to be left behind, along with the 1,200 women and children who had attached themselves to the British camp. This last measure was unpopular with all concerned, but Moore rightly pointed out that to take such a large number of women and children to war, would be to expose them 'to the greatest hardship and distress'. But regimental officers – who should have known better – turned a blind eye when the time came, and the women went anyway.

By 18 October Moore still had not moved, despite working sixteen hours a day in an attempt to get the army into shape, as he informed Castlereagh:

'In none of the departments is there any want of zeal, but in some of the important ones, there is much want of experience, and perhaps even of ability. This applies particularly to the Commissariat, few of whose members have ever seen an army in the field.'

In fact, Moore had little direct control over the Commissariat, which, as a civilian outfit tasked with procuring and distributing the army's rations, was answerable to the Treasury Department in London. His comments regarding its innocence of war, however, were well-founded, Commissariat officials being, for the most part, untrained clerks. In general, then, Moore, the consummate professional, was both baffled and astounded at the nonchalance and naivety by which he was surrounded: 'They talked of going into Spain as if going into Hyde Park', he commented. Then, to cap it all, a consultation with Portuguese engineers convinced the general that the route he had selected for his advance was unsuitable for cavalry and artillery. There seemed nothing for it, but to take the very unmilitary step of dividing his force and marching into the unknown at the head of the infantry, while Sir John Hope took the guns and horsemen on a lengthy detour, with orders to rendezvous once the Spanish interior had been made. Baird would have to catch up as best he could.

Finally, on 27 October, all was ready, and Moore quit Lisbon. He led an inexperienced, ill-fitted, ill-financed army along unfit roads, into an undeveloped, unfriendly country. His force was too small and too fragmented to achieve much unaided, yet his Spanish allies, whom he believed to be on the verge of victory, were in fact, on the brink of defeat. What awaited the British then, was not the opportunity to assist in a glorious triumph, but a lonely encounter with an enemy superior in skill and numbers, led by an acknowledged genius in war. Moore, meanwhile, was still preoccupied with getting to the front: 'If we get over this march,' he commented in all innocence, 'nothing after will appear difficult.'

On 1 November, Sir John crossed the River Tagus and led his foot soldiers into Spain, over roads which were, in the event, perfectly fit for horses and heavy guns. It was too late to call Hope back, however. He had already embarked on his pointless march through the province of Estremadura. Meanwhile, Moore decided to head for Salamanca, some 150 miles north-west of Madrid, there to await Hope and Baird before taking his place in the Spanish line of battle. Four days later, however, Sir John received the alarming news that General Castaños, far from awaiting a junction with his force, was actually marching away from him, towards a solo encounter with the French. Feeling increasingly isolated, Moore sent a message to Hope, begging him to hurry forward the guns, but to avoid approaching Madrid, which he rightly guessed to be the enemy's primary object.

On 13 November Moore arrived at Salamanca, but more bad news was waiting: Napoleon had arrived to take personal command of the French, unleashing a devastating offensive and driving all before him. Next day, Sir John learned that the Emperor had advanced as far as Valladolid, a mere seventy miles from his position. Meanwhile, a letter from Castlereagh arrived, ordering Moore to put himself under the command of a Spanish commander-in-chief, should the Supreme *Junta* decide to appoint one! The tragi-comedy was heightened further by John Hookham Frere, British ambassador at Madrid, who, seemingly impervious to the catastrophe unfolding about him, wrote to Moore, assuring him of the Spanish will to resist. Sir John, however, was already despairing of his allies, who seemed content to talk of resistance, while welcoming Napoleon, like a guest, to their capital. He replied to Frere's letter, informing the ambassador that unless the Spanish armies concentrated and presented a unified front, they risked destruction piecemeal. As for his own army, it remained scattered and unsupported, and in this vulnerable situation risked annihilation by superior French forces.

Meanwhile, Moore's assessment of the danger facing the Spanish proved all too accurate; within a matter of hours, word came that General Blake[5] had been defeated at Espinosa, losing 3,000 men, six guns, and all his baggage.

Feeling increasingly isolated, Sir John contacted Frere once more, to express incredulity at the unfolding fiasco:

> 'The imbecility of the Spanish Government exceeds belief ... I am in communication with no one Spanish army; nor am I acquainted with the intentions of the Spanish Government or any of its generals ... In the meantime the French are within four marches of me, whilst my army is only assembling: in what numbers they are I cannot learn ... If things are to continue in this state, the ruin of the Spanish cause and the defeat of their armies is inevitable; and it will become my duty to consider alone the safety of the British army and to take steps to withdraw it from a situation where, without the possibility of doing good, it is exposed to certain defeat.'

It seemed ridiculous to Moore that before his army had concentrated – let alone fired a shot in anger – it was faced with the possibility of headlong retreat. Meanwhile, 300 miles to the north-west, General Sir David Baird had only just got clear of Corunna and struck the trail for Salamanca. Baird – 'a bloody old bad-tempered Scotchman' according to one of his subordinates – was accompanied by 9,000 foot soldiers and 3,000 horsemen: the latter comprising two hussar brigades under Lord Henry Paget. Baird's troops had been cooped up in the holds of their ships in Corunna harbour for two weeks, before the Spaniards finally gave them permission to land on 4 November. The official reason for this delay, given by the Galician authorities, was that Baird's disembarkation had to be authorised by the Supreme *Junta* at Madrid. Unofficially, however, the impoverished Galicians – having been stripped of supplies by their own soldiers – were embarrassed to admit that they were no longer in a position to supply their allies.

By 19 November, with little aid from the Spaniards, Baird had got as far as Astorga, roughly halfway between Corunna and Salamanca, though, as he wrote to Moore, he was far from sure why he was there:

'As it could never be intended by the British
Government that our army should engage in the
defence of this country unaided and unsupported by
any Spanish force, I confess, my dear Sir John, I begin
to be at a loss to discover an object at this moment in
Spain.'

Baird was not the only one 'at a loss', for Moore,
languishing at Salamanca in an information-vacuum, was just
as baffled, writing tetchily to Castlereagh:

'If I had had a conception of the weakness of the
Spanish armies, the depleted state of the country, and
the apparent apathy of the people and the selfish
imbecility of the Government I should certainly have
been in no hurry to enter Spain or to have approached
the scene of action, until the army was united . . .[the
advance into Spain] may prove the worst thing I could
have done.'

On 26 November, Moore received a further missive from
Frere, informing him that, in consequence of Napoleon's
continued advance, the Supreme *Junta* was about to flee
Madrid for the relative safety of Cordoba. Frere made it clear,
however, that he expected Moore to remain and fight, adding
that a British retreat would 'sink the hearts of the whole
country'. Moore replied on the instant, pointing out his
increasingly precarious situation, and stating his opinion that,
from the military standpoint, an immediate retreat on Portugal
was the only sensible thing to do. He conceded, however, that
there were diplomatic niceties to be observed, and was fully
aware that he was expected to stay put and make a *beau geste*
on behalf of the British government. He therefore agreed to
accommodate Frere – for the time being – and dashed off the
following lines to Baird:

'I see my situation and that of the army I command in
as unfavourable a light as you or anyone can do. But
. . . it is our business to make every effort to unite here
and to obey our orders and the wishes of the country

to aid the Spaniards as far as it lies in our power. It
would never do to retreat without making the attempt.'

Two days later, Moore received news from Charles Stuart,
Acting Minister at Madrid (Frere having fled), of a crushing
defeat sustained by the Spanish army under General Castaños
at Tudela, on the north-eastern approaches to the capital.
Now there was nothing to stop Napoleon marching on Madrid
– or Salamanca, for that matter. 'As long as Castaños' army
remained there was hope,' Moore confided to his journal, 'but
I now see none.' Retreat was now the only option, and Moore
summoned his staff to inform them of his decision. Many
murmured their disapproval, but Sir John snapped:

> 'I have not called you together to request your counsel
> or to induce you to commit yourselves by giving any
> opinion on the subject. I take the responsibility entirely
> upon myself. I only require that you will immediately
> prepare for carrying it into effect.'

He then countermanded Baird's instructions to advance,
ordering him to fall back on Corunna:

> 'My Dear Sir David, I have received this evening
> dispatches from Mr Stuart at Madrid, announcing the
> defeat and dispersion of Castaños' army. The French
> in Spain are estimated at 80,000 men and 30,000 are
> expected in the course of a week . . . I have, therefore,
> determined to retreat upon Portugal with the corps I
> have here; and if possible, with Hope's corps, if by
> forced marches he can join me.'

Hope made the junction with Moore on 5 December, the
day on which Sir John received an enthusiastic report from the
Supreme *Junta*, claiming to describe the 'true' situation: the
people of Madrid had risen up in arms; 80,000 Spanish
regulars were marching to their assistance; the fate of the
French was sealed, etc., etc. Moore continued his preparations
for retreat. Then, at 7.30 p.m., a messenger from Frere
arrived at headquarters – a French *émigré* officer, by the name
of Colonel Venault Charmilly. Moore had met this man on a

previous occasion and had taken an instant dislike to him –
with some justification, as it happens, for Charmilly was a
shady character, implicated in all manner of dark, dirty
dealings. Now he was the bearer of an important letter from
Ambassador Frere. The contents of this epistle exuberantly
echoed that of the *Junta*'s, claiming that the population of
Madrid was afire with patriotic zeal, and ready to defend their
city to the last. Frere, however, was no longer in the capital –
having decamped to Talavera – and it was clear that he was
basing his assertions largely on Charmilly's testimony. Frere
concluded his letter with the words, 'I consider the fate of
Spain as depending absolutely for the present upon the
decision which you may adopt.'

Sir John stared at these words intently, while Charmilly
enthused, flapping about like a fanatic: 'It is now too late,'
growled Moore, 'I am very busy tonight.' And so it proved.
For that night, Sir John did not sleep. Instead, he turned the
dilemma over and over in his mind. Should he remain or
should he quit? Was he being presented with the truth or
another pack of lies?

With dawn came his decision: Baird would be recalled, the
British army would unite, and the whole force would make a
strike in support of the reported insurrection at Madrid. Thus,
Sir John informed Baird of yet another change in plan:

> 'The people of Madrid, it is said, are enthusiastic and
> desperate; and certainly at this moment do resist the
> French – the good which may result from this it is
> impossible to say; I can neither trust to it, nor can I
> altogether despise it. If the flame catches elsewhere,
> and becomes at all general, the best results may be
> expected; if confined to Madrid, that town will be
> sacrificed, and all will be as bad, or worse than ever.
> In short, what is passing at Madrid may be decisive of
> the fate of Spain; and we must be at hand to aid and
> to take advantage of whatever happens. The wishes of
> our country, and our duty, demand this of us, with
> whatever risk it may be attended. I mean to proceed

bridle in hand; for if the bubble bursts, and Madrid falls, we shall have a run for it. . . '

At noon, Charmilly appeared before Sir John once more, this time his mood was solemn. He knew nothing of Sir John's change of heart, and hesitantly gave up a second letter from Frere, which, he explained, the Ambassador had ordered him not to pass on unless absolutely necessary. Moore snatched the missive from his hand, ripped it open, and read Frere's message in amazement:

> 'In the event, which I did not wish to presuppose, of your continuing the determination already announced to me of retiring with the army under your command, I have to request that Colonel Charmilly, who is the bearer of this, and whose intelligence has already been referred to, may be previously examined before a council of war.'

In essence, the letter was a cheap ploy to undermine Moore's authority by threatening to give Charmilly's claims of Spanish resistance a public voice, thus compromising the general in front of his subordinates. Considering the bold decision he had just made, the irony was not lost on Moore. He remained silent, however, his features frozen in a half-smile. Then he calmly ordered his adjutant-general to have Charmilly escorted from camp. The Frenchman, still in the dark as to Sir John's intentions, returned to Frere in a state of high dudgeon, prompting the following, petulant note from the diplomat:

> '. . . if the British army had been sent abroad for the express object of doing the utmost possible mischief to the cause of Spain, short of actually firing upon the Spanish troops, they would have most completely fulfilled their purpose by carrying out exactly the measures which they have taken.'

Meanwhile, Moore's young staff merrily prepared for the coming adventure, while the general meditated on the step he was about to take. Although he wished to believe that the citizens of Madrid were making a stand and that an opportunity for glory beckoned, he simply could not be sure that, this time, he was not being lied to. He already had ample proof that no one with a vested interest in the affairs of Spain could be trusted: Castlereagh was vague, the *Junta* false, Frere deluded, and Charmilly disreputable. Certain of nothing but his army's desire for a fight, he informed Castlereagh of his plans, concluding with the assurance that he would:

> '... never abandon the cause as long as it holds out a chance of success – but you must be sensible that the ground may be, in an instant, cut from under me. Madrid may fall and I shall be left to contend with very superior forces indeed.'

Unbeknown to Moore, a French bulletin had already announced the fall of Madrid and its occupation by the Emperor's troops.

Moore learned of Madrid's fate on 9 December with the return of Colonel Thomas Graham, who had been sent off in the direction of the capital several days before on a fact-finding mission. Despite this catastrophe, however, Graham had also offered a glimmer of hope, by informing Moore of the continued stand of patriots in the south, and an apparent defeat inflicted on French forces by the defenders of Saragossa, the Aragonese city which had been defiantly resisting assaults since June. According to Graham, official reports spoke of heavy French columns descending upon Saragossa on 1 December, and of a major battle, in which the enemy was repulsed with great loss; in truth a small force under Marshal Moncey had approached and, after a brief exchange of gunfire and a skirmish in which four Frenchmen were killed, a tactical withdrawal had been made in order to await reinforcements prior to the re-commencement of the siege. The British, however, were deceived yet again and eager to do something, if only for the sake of honour, Sir John made the monumentally brave decision to push ahead with his advance, in the hope of assisting the southern rebels by drawing off Napoleon's forces in his direction: 'I shall threaten the French communications and create a diversion,' he declared, 'if the Spaniards can avail themselves of it. . . '

On 13 December, the British filed out of Salamanca, heading east for the front. They marched for two days without anything of note occurring; then, a captured French despatch was placed in Moore's hands. It was delivered by a certain Captain Waters, who had bought it for twenty dollars in a village near Segovia, from peasants who had murdered the courier. It was a note from Napoleon's chief of staff, Marshal Berthier, to Marshal Soult, commanding the Emperor's II Corps. Apart from giving a breakdown of French dispositions, it also stated as fact, that the British were fleeing back towards Portugal.

Moore could not believe his luck; the French knew nothing of his whereabouts, yet he now knew of theirs in detail. He immediately changed his line of march, directing his men to make a 130-mile thrust to the north, in order to attack Soult's isolated corps which was evidently concentrated around Carrion. It was a risky undertaking, should Napoleon discover his plan, but Moore was willing to take a gamble in support of the resistance movement and for the sake of the Anglo-Spanish alliance. On 15 December, he informed Castlereagh of the undertaking, declaring that, 'It will be very agreeable to give a wipe to such a Corps.' Moore realised, however, that the coup would be of little value if the Spaniards failed to make good use of it:

> '. . . even if I beat Soult, unless the victory had the effect
> to rouse the Spaniards and to give their leaders ability,
> it will be attended with no other advantage than the
> character it will attach to the British arms.'

By 20 December Moore was at Mayorga, having pushed the pace with forced marches of eleven hours per day, and here he was at last joined by Baird. Next day, the combined British force marched through thunder, lightning, and pouring rain towards their *rencontre* with Soult, now a mere 40 miles away. Riding ahead of the infantry were the light cavalry of Lord Henry Paget's hussar brigades. As evening fell, they neared the village of Sahagun, several miles in advance of Soult's lines. The place was occupied by 500 French horsemen – an advanced post of the marshal's army, under the command of General Debelle. During the course of a bitter cold night, the rain having given way to snow, Sahagun was outflanked by 400 troopers from the 10th and 15th Hussars, commanded by Paget in person. At dawn, the British attacked, with striking results recorded by Captain Gordon of the 15th:

> 'The shock was terrible. Horses and men were overthrown, and a shriek of terror, intermixed with oaths, groans, and prayers for mercy, issued from the whole extent of their front.'

A few minutes later and it was all over: 120 Frenchmen were killed, 150 taken prisoner and the rest scattered; first blood to the British: 'It was a handsome thing and well done,' commented Moore.

Next day, Moore halted the army and made his headquarters at Sahagun. His infantry, though eager to fight, were worn down with heavy marching and needed rest before going into action. The whole of the 22nd, therefore, was given over to repose and last-minute preparations for the final push. Next day, with snow falling thick and fast, Moore opened his journal and wrote:

> 'This night we march in two columns on Carrion, where, I believe, some of the French are . . . we start at eight in the evening.'

Notes

1. Lieutenant-General Sir Harry Burrard, though frequently described in the literature as being seventy-three years old, was, according to Sir Charles Oman, and more recently in Philip J. Haythornthwaite's *Who Was Who in the Napoleonic Wars*, born in 1755, making him fifty-three years old in 1808.

2. Sometimes described as a geriatric in the literature, General Sir Hew Dalrymple was born in 1750, according to Philip J. Haythornthwaite, making him fifty-eight years old in 1808. Wellesley, incidentally, was almost forty, and Moore almost forty-seven.

3. Although the Convention of Cintra was lampooned in Britain as the very acme of dishonour, it was approved by both Wellesley and Moore as the best way forward, once the initiative had been lost by Burrard in the final moments at Vimiero.

4. Moore, James, *Narrative of the Campaign of the British Army in Spain.*

5. Joachim Blake (1759–1827) was a Spaniard of Irish descent, and one of the country's foremost generals.

The Bubble Bursts

It was bitter cold at Sahagun on the evening of 23 December, and the snow, lying several inches deep, spread a shroud for the corpses of those killed in the recent cavalry clash, the iron-hard ground denying them burial. Moore's men, however, were hot for action, as they formed up for the advance on Carrion, their mood bold and bullish: 'Every heart beat with joy,' remembered the anonymous 'Soldier of the 71st', 'We were all under arms and formed to attack the enemy. Every mouth breathed hope.' Moore, too, was poised for the daring enterprise and, having issued all the necessary orders, took up his pen and addressed these lines to Frere:

> 'I march this night to Carrion and the next day to Saldaña, to attack the corps under Marshal Soult ...The movement I am making is of the most dangerous kind. I not only risk to be surrounded every moment by superior forces, but to have my communication intercepted with the Galicias. I wish it be apparent to the whole world, as it is to every individual of the army, that we have done everything in our power in support of the Spanish cause; and that we do not abandon it, until long after the Spaniards had abandoned us.'

Thus it was in an atmosphere of fervent anticipation, during which, according to Benjamin Harris of the 95th

Regiment, the men 'longed for blood', that Moore and his army awaited the coming of night.

But shortly after dusk had fallen – and a mere hour before Moore himself was due to quit headquarters – a messenger arrived bearing a despatch from General Romana at Mansilla; Spanish agents were reporting powerful French forces pouring out of Madrid, their leading elements crossing the Guadarrama Mountains and heading north for the plains of Leon. Apparently, Moore's design to divert the French juggernaut from its course of conquest had succeeded – and only too well – for Napoleon, finally aware of his presence (thanks to a warning from Soult), was bearing down upon his pocket-sized army[1] at the head of 40,000 picked troops. At last, Moore's 'bubble' had burst. Isolated, outnumbered, threatened with encirclement and annihilation, it was now time to 'run for it'.

Thus, within minutes, the strategic situation had changed completely and Moore could no longer afford the luxury of a swipe at Soult. Nevertheless, he had scored a success of sorts, as he explained in his reply to Romana:

> 'My movement has, in some degree, answered its object, as it has drawn the enemy from other projects and will give the South more time to prepare. With such a force as mine, I can pretend to do no more. It would be losing this army to Spain and to England, to persevere in my march on Soult; who, if posted strongly, might wait or if not, would retire and draw me on until the corps from Madrid got behind me: in short, single-handed, I cannot pretend to contend with the superior numbers the French can bring against me.'

His message ended with an acknowledgement of Romana's 'zeal and activity', coupled with an appeal to the Spanish general to remain, for the time being, at Mansilla (in order to 'blind the enemy'); Moore himself would make for Astorga and the comparative safety of the Galician mountains.

The advance on Carrion, therefore, was cancelled and the troops – who were offered no explanation – were stood down and sent back to their quarters confused and crestfallen.

General Charles Stewart, in command of one of Lord Paget's two cavalry brigades, noted the change that came over the army the moment the sortie was abandoned:

> 'It would be no easy matter to describe the effect which this unlooked-for event produced upon the army. Troops, who had panted to meet the enemy and who, but an hour ago, were full of life and confidence, suddenly appeared like men whose hopes were withered. Few complained but all retired to their quarters in a state of sullen silence, which indicated more powerfully perhaps than words, the mortification under which they laboured.'

A young Irish recruit expressed the general mood a little more bluntly:

> 'And won't we be allowed to fight? By Saint Patrick, we'd beat them so easy, the General means to march us to death, and fight them after!'

Meanwhile, the army's advanced guard, having already set off for Carrion, had to be recalled. Forbidden to speak, these troops had tramped in silence for miles through thick snow, fully expecting to be in action by dawn. When, at last, the order came to retire, they found themselves – to their complete astonishment – no longer at the head of an advancing army, but the tail-end of a retreating one: 'I expected a battle, a victory, and plenty of provisions,' observed the anonymous 'Private of the 42nd', 'but that night we commenced the retreat.'

According to Benjamin Harris of the 95th, the order to retire came at 2.00 a. m.:

> 'General Craufurd, in command of the brigade, was riding in front when I observed a dragoon come spurring furiously along the road to meet us. He delivered a letter to the General, who, the moment he

read a few lines, turned round in his saddle and thundered out the word to halt. A few minutes more and we were all turned to the right about and were retracing our steps of the night before. The contents of that epistle served to furnish our men with many a surmise during this retrograde movement. When we again neared Sahagun, wives and children came rushing into the ranks and embraced the husbands and fathers they expected never to see again.'

When daylight broke on 24 December, Napoleon was a mere sixty miles from Moore, but having dragged his army over the Guadarramas in the teeth of a brutal blizzard, during which, according to Sir Charles Oman, 'a considerable number of men died of cold and fatigue', the Emperor declared a day of rest. Meanwhile, Sir John, in the words of his devoted brother James, 'was silently but busily occupied in preparing to retire; which, in the presence of an enemy, is the most difficult of all military operations. . . '

Moore's first objective was to pass the natural barrier of the River Esla without interference from the French. Although three possible crossing points existed, he immediately ruled out the bridge at Mansilla and the ford at Valencia. The former place was occupied by Romana, whose men had stripped the surrounding country of supplies, while the latter was deemed unsuitable for the passage of a whole army, especially as the Esla was in flood. This left the bridge at Castrogonzalo, some fifty miles to the south. Reached via Mayorga and Valderas, this bridge had the added benefit of being close to Benavente, a fortified town and major army depot, on the main road to Galicia. However, in order to delay the French pursuit for as long as possible, all three positions would have to be secured. Baird, therefore, was detailed to seize the ford at Valencia, while Romana was requested to 'keep a strong corps at Mansilla, to defend the bridge there'. As an afterthought, Moore added:

'You will, I suppose, think it right when I am passed, to order the boats upon the river to be destroyed. I have only to repeat my request, that Astorga and its neighbourhood may be left for the British troops, together with the passage into the Galicias.'

Having thus detached Baird's 1st Division and sent it west to Valencia, Moore proceeded to parcel his army up further: the 2nd and 3rd Divisions, under Generals Hope and Fraser, respectively, would form the vanguard, spearheading the march south-west to Castrogonzalo; the 4th or Reserve Division, under General Sir Edward Paget (Lord Henry Paget's younger brother) would remain at Sahagun for twenty-four hours in order to cover this departure; the 1st and 2nd Flank or Light Brigades, under Colonel Robert Craufurd and Major-General Karl Alten, would also linger, providing a rearguard for the Reserve; as for Lord Paget's two light cavalry brigades, they would screen all these movements from the French, keeping Soult in the dark for as long as possible, by aggressively pushing patrols towards Carrion. They would be the last to leave, pulling out of Sahagun at nightfall on the 25th, several hours after the Light Brigades had quit. Moore elected to march with the Reserve.

At noon, the leading columns began their retreat, 'melancholy and dejected', according to the 'Soldier of the 71st', 'sinking under extreme cold and fatigue, as if the very elements had conspired against us.' Each man bore a burden of at least 60 lb (27 kg), which included his musket, bayonet, ammunition, blanket and knapsack. The latter, a rigid, box-like affair, secured by tight straps over the shoulders and chest, dug into the soldier's spine and restricted his breathing. It was at this point that the troops, according to Harris:

> '...suddenly recollected that this was Christmas Eve ...Many talked of home and recollected previous Christmas Eves in Old England, shedding tears as they spoke of the relatives never to be seen again...'

Christmas Day dawned cruelly cold as those left in Sahagun braced themselves for the trials which lay ahead. Quartermaster Sergeant William Surtees, a comrade of Harris' in the 2nd Battalion, 95th, was none too optimistic:

'Winter had now completely set in ... the face of the country being covered with deep snow, the weather was unusually severe. Our prospect, therefore, was by no means a pleasant one. To commence a retreat in front of a greatly superior force, and with the probability that other French armies might be before us, and intercept our retreat upon the sea, which was distant from us nearly 250 miles, with the country in our rear being already exhausted of everything that could contribute to our support, and with such excessively bad weather to perform the retreat in, rendered it, I may say, as unpleasant a situation as troops could well be placed in.'

Moore's assessment was hardly less sobering. Before his departure, Sir John opened his journal for what would be the last time, recording these words for posterity:

'I was aware that I risked infinitely too much; but something, I thought, was to be risked for the honour of the service and to make it apparent that we stuck to the Spaniards long after they themselves had given up their cause as lost ... If we can steal two marches upon the French we shall be quiet; if we are followed close, I must stop and offer battle. At this season of the year, in a country without fuel, it is impossible to bivouac; the villages are small, which obliges us to march thus by corps in succession. Our retreat, therefore, becomes much more difficult.'

As if on cue, the heavens opened as Moore and the Reserve Division decamped, heaving down an icy torrent which drenched the men and turned their trail into a mire of mud and slush.

The last foot soldiers to file out of town were the light infantrymen of Robert Craufurd's 1st Flank Brigade. A martinet of the first order, known as 'Black Bob' to his men, Craufurd sat astride his horse – stoical, immovable and soaked to the skin – glowering at the troops as they trudged past. Benjamin Harris noted Craufurd's mood:

> 'He did not like to see us going rearwards and many of
> us judged by his severe look and scowling eye that
> there must be something wrong ...."Keep your ranks
> there, men!" he said, spurring his horse towards some
> riflemen who were avoiding a small rivulet. "Keep
> your ranks and move on. No straggling from the main
> body!"'

But many men were so worn with hunger, cold and
exhaustion, they were almost dead on their feet and literally
sleepwalking.

And so the rearguard pressed on without food or rest,
dogging the tracks of the leading columns and discovering
ominous signs of apparent haste and disorder: an overturned
Commissariat wagon abandoned with all its contents; a
sergeant of the 92nd Highlanders, broken by fatigue and left
by his comrades to die in the road. 'As we passed,' recorded
Harris bleakly, 'no one stopped to offer him any assistance.'

Back in Sahagun, however, cavalry commander Charles
Stewart had cause to be satisfied with events so far:

> 'Everything ... was done with perfect regularity -- the
> columns made good their march, the one to Valencia,
> the other to Castrogonzalo, without molestation -- and
> at the appointed hour, the rearguard withdrew, leaving
> the enemy ignorant that a retreat had ever been in
> contemplation.'

And much of this was thanks to the 2,500 sabres of the five
regiments of hussars. In fact, so energetically had Paget's
cavalry executed its task of containing Soult, the marshal had
begun to fear he might be the target of a general onslaught.
Nevertheless, from 21–24 December, the hussars had suffered
terrible hardships: 'Some of the men got frostbitten,' recorded
Sir John Slade in his journal, 'and one poor woman, a
trumpeter's wife, died from the cold.'[2] Kept constantly in
action, one cavalryman recalled going fifty hours without food,
and another that he did not remove his boots for three days.

It was with some relief then, when, on 25 December, the advanced posts were at last called in and preparations made to follow the infantry. Slade's journal continues:

'Marched at three in the morning back to Sahagun, but how very different was the treatment to that which we received on advancing! No more ringing of bells; no longer did the air resound with "Long live the good English!" All the shops were shut and not anything to be got for love or money. I may truly say it was the most unpleasant Christmas Day I ever passed.'

Later that day, at about 4.00 p.m., Captain Alexander Gordon of the 15th Hussars, was ordered to quit his advanced post at the hamlet of Villa Lebrin and fall back on Sahagun:

'We passed over the ground where the action of the 21st took place,' he wrote, 'and I observed several corpses unburied, "a prey to dogs and birds." The peasants had stripped them, and it was reported that the body of a female was found amongst the number ... We arrived at Sahagun just in time to join the mess, where all the officers of the regiment, except those absent on duty, were assembled to celebrate the day; but the mirth and jollity usually prevalent at this season were considerably damped by reflection on the critical situation in which we were placed.'

The danger of the situation was exacerbated by the sudden appearance of typhus (a highly contagious louse-borne disease, which thrives in the wake of squalor and wretchedness; symptoms vary, ranging from headaches, fever and delirium, to abscesses, gangrene, dysentery and even death). In his journal, Gordon tells of a certain Lieutenant Penrice, dangerously ill with the disease, who had to be abandoned at Sahagun for want of adequate transport:

'Lord Paget left a letter addressed to the commanding officer of any French troops which might enter the town, requesting kind treatment for Penrice, and offering, in the event of his recovery, to give any officer of the same rank taken prisoner on the 21st in exchange for him.'[3]

Meanwhile, Benjamin Harris and the men of Craufurd's brigade continued their hike to Castrogonzalo:

> 'Night came down without – and here I speak for myself and those around me – without our having tasted food or having halted. All night long we continued this dreadful march. Men began to look into each other's faces and ask the question, "Are we ever to be halted again?"'

Notes

1. According to Napier, Moore's total effective strength on 19 December was 23,583. See Appendix XXV in Napier, William, *History of the War in the Peninsula*.
2. Quotations from Slade's Journal are from Mollo, John, *The Prince's Dolls*.
3. Penrice recovered and was sent home in 1809.

The Race for Benavente

On the morning of 26 December, Moore's redcoats continued their slog to Castrogonzalo, 'over miserable roads, through an exhausted country, and exposed to greater hardships than it has frequently fallen to the lot of British soldiers to endure.'[1] The weather was truly appalling and, as the men marched, a black and bitter spirit seeped into their skins with the ice-cold rain. Why were they retreating from an enemy they had previously punished with ease? Where were the much vaunted Spanish armies? And why were not all local men under arms, ready to repel the invader? The British soldiers – still in the dark as to the wider strategic picture – felt themselves betrayed on all sides, as the 'Soldier of the 71st' commented:

> 'The poor Spaniards had little to expect from such men as these who blamed them for their inactivity. Everyone found at home was looked upon as a traitor to his country. "The British are here to fight for the liberty of Spain, and why is not every Spaniard under arms and fighting?" Such was the common language of the soldiers.'

It was at this point that Moore's freezing, famished men – unable to wait for the floundering Commissariat to distribute rations – began taking food by force, as they tramped through the wretched, roadside villages. Now the very people they had been sent to succour began to suffer at their hands. General Charles Stewart tells how the Spaniards – at once terrified and incensed:

> '...abandoned their houses as the British army approached, locking their doors and concealing the little stock of provisions of which they were possessed ...These things increased the irritation under which the troops already laboured. They began to look upon the Spaniards as enemies and treat them as people unworthy of consideration. This was severely retaliated by an enraged peasantry; and scenes of violence and bloodshed too frequently occurred.'

While the main column crept south, over execrable roads and through filthy weather, Baird's 1st Division made good progress and on the 26th waded through the rising waters of the Esla at Valencia. The river was fordable despite the flood, but the men were, nevertheless, obliged to wallow waist-deep in liquid mud upon reaching the far bank: 'There had been a pretty strong flood in the river,' recorded the 'Private of the 42nd':

> 'At the ford we had to fix our ammunition on the top of our knapsacks, to prevent it from getting wet in fording the river: this was very disagreeable work at that inclement season ...all of us did not escape a ducking.'

The passage completed, Baird took up his position as ordered and dashed off a despatch to Romana at Mansilla, urging him to blow the bridge before the enemy could make use of it. But Romana, 'a very good excellent man but no general'[2] – left the bridge intact, entrusting its defence to 3,000 sickly Spanish soldiers (augmented by four cannon), while he retired, with the remainder of his force, on the nearby city of Leon.

Napoleon, meanwhile, was on the move once more, pushing his pursuing force of 40,000 from Tordesillas to the banks of the Esla, in what his soldiers came to call 'the race for Benavente'. The Emperor's strike was spearheaded by the cavalry of the Imperial Guard, led by his former *aide-de-camp*, General Charles Lefebvre-Desnouëttes. These élite horsemen – known as 'The Invincibles' after their battle-winning charge at Austerlitz three years before – had already begun prodding Moore's rearguard, keeping Paget's hussars busy. Concurrently, the fog of war was lifting for Marshal Soult, who, realising that he was not to be assailed after all, had at last bestirred himself. Aiming to outflank Moore to the north, thus cutting off his retreat into the Galicias, he set off for Astorga, opting for the direct route via the bridge at Mansilla, so conveniently left intact by Romana. Meanwhile, cavalry scouts of Marshal Ney's VI Corps had stumbled across Paget's path at Mayorga.

Lord Henry William Paget, future Earl of Uxbridge, Marquess of Anglesey, and Waterloo hero, was probably the best British cavalry commander of the period. Forty years old in 1808, he was described by a fellow officer as 'magnificent and tireless', while according to one of his hussars, 'he was almost idolised – ay, worshipped ...It was a common expression amongst the troopers that they would follow him to hell.' As the morning of the 26th progressed, Paget's whole force – hugging the banks of the Cea, a tributary of the Esla, and paddling down roads two feet deep in mud – came within sight of Mayorga, roughly halfway between Sahagun and Castrogonzalo. Captain Gordon of the 15th Hussars, tells how, upon their approach, they:

> '...found that town occupied by the enemy and learned that the baggage of the cavalry, which had been sent forward the day before, was captured by them. Lord Paget immediately pushed on with the Tenth, followed by the Fifteenth. Our left squadron was ordered to support the troops of horse artillery attached to the brigade, and the rattling of the guns as we galloped through the streets completed the panic of the inhabitants, who were making the most doleful lamentations.'

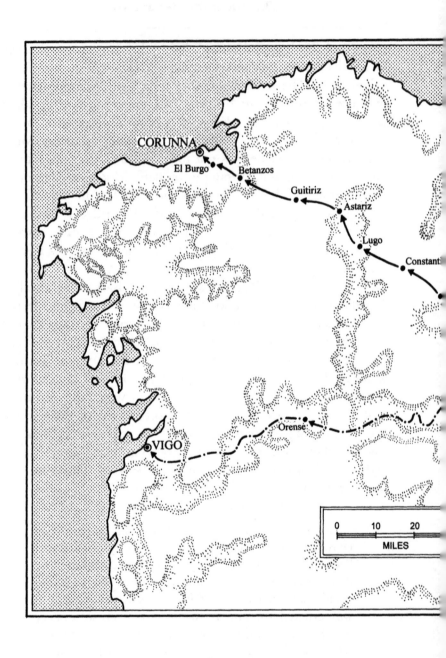

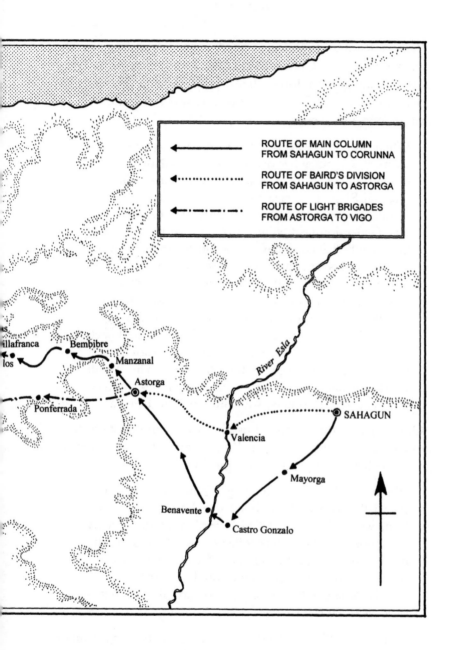

ROUTE OF MAIN COLUMN
FROM SAHAGUN TO CORUNNA

ROUTE OF BAIRD'S DIVISION
FROM SAHAGUN TO ASTORGA

ROUTE OF LIGHT BRIGADES
FROM ASTORGA TO VIGO

River Esla

Villafranca
los
Bembibre
Manzanal
Astorga
Ponferrada
SAHAGUN
Valencia
Mayorga
Benavente
Castro Gonzalo

Chapter 3

Paget's leading squadrons were soon skirmishing in the streets with the 15th Chasseurs à Cheval and, after some fierce fighting, managed to force them from their positions, then evict them entirely. The fight, however, was not quite over, as Gordon soon discovered:

> 'When we got clear of the town, two squadrons of *chasseurs à cheval* were discovered, formed on a rising ground about a mile distant. Lord Paget directed General Slade to attack them with a squadron of the Tenth, supported by the remainder of the regiment. The General moved off at a trot but had not advanced far when he halted to have some alteration made in the length of his stirrups. An *aide-de-camp* was sent to inquire the cause of this delay, and the squadron was again put in motion; but the General's stirrups were not yet adjusted to his mind, and he halted again before they had advanced 100 yards ... Lord Paget, whose patience was by this time quite exhausted, then ordered Colonel Leigh to take the lead. The Tenth charged gallantly, routed the enemy, and took between forty and fifty prisoners, with little loss on their part.'

Once again, the British hussars had demonstrated their complete ascendancy over the French and Paget himself, in writing of this action, stated in typically blunt prose:

> 'We attacked them again, they again fired, by which they killed two and wounded one horse. They stood firm, we broke them, killed several, wounded twenty and took prisoners, one officer, 100 men and fifty horses. *We* are in the greatest favour. The army is retreating and it is high time it should, for there are no Spaniards and lots of French. We are all well but a good deal harassed.'

As for 'Jack' Slade, Paget never forgave the unfortunate general for his dilatory behaviour at Mayorga, pronouncing him 'a bungler' and 'a damned stupid fellow'.

By late afternoon, as dusk descended, the cavalry had entered Valderas, about ten miles from Castrogonzalo.

Exhausted by their efforts (they had been in the saddle for thirteen hours), both men and horses were in desperate need of rest. However, the place was bursting with rowdy, riotous infantrymen committing, in the words of historian and campaign veteran, William Napier, 'disgraceful excesses' and billets were almost impossible to find. Dissatisfaction, it seemed, was filtering down from Moore's own, largely inexperienced staff, with the result that, as Napier points out:

> 'Many regimental officers neglected their duty, and what with dislike to a retreat, the severity of the weather, and the inexperience of the army, the previous fine discipline of the troops was broken down.'

Meanwhile, in the gathering gloom and with the rain still falling in torrents, the leading elements of Hope's and Fraser's divisions finally marched into Castrogonzalo, over the bridge, and onto the Benavente side of the Esla. The 43rd Regiment was detailed to guard the crossing and two privates – John Walton and Richard Jackson – were posted on the Castrogonzalo bank, on the brow of a hill which commanded the approaches to the bridge. Their orders were that should the French appear, one must stand firm while the other raised the alarm. Some time later, under cover of darkness and the continuing deluge, a number of French horsemen successfully penetrated Paget's cavalry screen and – pausing only to seize some women and plunder – stealthily advanced upon the bridge. Napier described what followed:

> 'Jackson fired, but was overtaken and received twelve or fourteen sabre cuts in an instant; nevertheless, he came staggering on and gave the signal, while Walton, with equal resolution, stood his ground and wounded several of the assailants, who retired leaving him unhurt, but with his cap, knapsack, belts and musket cut in above twenty places, his bayonet bent double, bloody to the hilt and notched like a saw.'

An alternative account of the 'remarkable display of courage and discipline' described by Napier above, comes from Quartermaster Sergeant William Surtees. In charge of a quantity of baggage, Surtees was doggedly seeking his battalion's headquarters in the obscurity of a murky night. He had made the Benavente bank earlier in the evening, only to be told that the 2nd Battalion of the 95th were at Castro Pipa, back over the bridge, about a mile from Castrogonzalo. He was in the act of recrossing the Esla when:

> '...just as I reached the end of the bridge, I heard a shot immediately in my front. The 43rd Regiment guarded the bridge. It turned out to be a patrol of the enemy's cavalry who had come close to the top of the slope leading down to the bridge, and where a double sentry of the 43rd was posted. By some accident these two men were not loaded; the French dragoons were consequently permitted to come close up to them without their being able to give any alarm. One of them, however, run [sic] his bayonet into one of the Frenchmen's horses, and retreated, but the other was not only cut down with the sabre, but had a pistol fired at him, which was the report I had just heard. I saw the wounded man, who was severely hurt, but whether he survived or not I know not ...When I reached Castro Pipa, my commanding officer would scarcely credit the report I gave him, conceiving it impossible the French could be such near neighbours.'

At daybreak on 27 December, the hussars at Valderas found themselves enshrouded in a thick fog which, according to Captain Gordon:

> '...made it impossible to discern objects at the distance of a horse's length. The church bells sounded for a long time to give notice of a fire which had broken out in the town; it burned with great fury and caused considerable damage before it was extinguished ...Here we began to shoot the horses and mules which were lame or in other respects unfit for hard work. I counted about forty lying dead in the streets of this place; and at a subsequent period of the retreat, ten of these animals were destroyed, on a moderate computation, for every mile we marched.'

Gordon quit Valderas at 9.00 a.m. with his regiment and splashed through the sludge down the road to Castrogonzalo. Soon, however, he came across casualties of a different kind:

> 'Our route lay through several villages, which exhibited melancholy proofs of the shameful devastation committed by the infantry which had preceded us; we observed one in flames whilst we were at a considerable distance, and it was still burning when we passed through it. The inhabitants shouted, *"Vivan los Franceses!"* and we overtook some stragglers who had been stripped and maltreated by the Spaniards.'

The situation was not much better in Benavente. Upon their arrival in town, the first thing the men of the vanguard had done was hunt for alcohol. With little or no money of their own, some soldiers cut the buttons from their jackets and tried to pass them off as English coin, in a bid to buy liquor. Others made straight for the wine cellars, hauling barrels onto the streets and peppering them with musket-balls, in order to make holes from which the juice might flow, but the barrels simply split and the wine cascaded into the gutters whereupon the troops – desperate to escape their sufferings into the oblivion of intoxication – scooped the liquid up in their caps, mud and all. A drunken riot followed in short order. 'Indignant at the little assistance afforded them by the Spaniards,' wrote James Moore, the redcoats 'took the opportunity which the retreat afforded them of throwing off restraint . . .[and] acting too much as they pleased.'

Moore – who had been marching with the Reserve – was appalled at the scenes he witnessed upon entering Benavente. Still fuming over the unruly behaviour of the men on the march from Valderas, Sir John was now incandescent and lost no time announcing the fact in his General Orders:

> 'The Commander of the Forces has observed with concern, the extreme bad conduct of the troops at a moment when they are about to come into contact with the enemy, and when the greatest regularity and the best conduct are the most requisite . . . The

misbehaviour of the troops in the column which
marched by Valderas to this place, exceeds what he
could have believed of British soldiers. It is disgraceful
to the officers; as it strongly marks their negligence and
inattention.'

And in a counter-attack aimed at the growing ranks of
disaffected whisperers behind his back:

'It is impossible for the General to explain to his army
the motive for the movement he directs. The
Commander of the Forces can, however, assure the
army that he has made none since he left Salamanca
which he did not foresee, and was not prepared for;
and, as far as he is a judge, they have answered the
purposes for which they were intended ... When it is
proper to fight a battle he will do it; and he will choose
the time and place he thinks most fit: in the meantime
he begs the officers and soldiers of the army to attend
diligently to discharge their parts, and to leave to him
and to the general officers the decision of measures
which belong to them alone.'

Having given a literary lashing to his own men and officers,
Moore now addressed the shortcomings of his Spanish allies,
who, despite numerous declarations, had done nothing to
hinder Napoleon's progress. Furthermore, it had come to the
General's attention that, in some cases, Spaniards had even
provided requisites for the Emperor's army, which they had
denied to his own. Picking up his pen once more, he drafted
a letter to Romana, beginning with a lecture on military
strategy:

'My opinion is, that a battle is the game of Buonaparte,
not ours. We should, if followed, take defensive
positions in the mountains, where his cavalry can be of
no use to him; and there either engage him in an
unequal contest with us, oblige him to employ a
considerable corps to watch us, or to retire upon
Madrid: in which last case we should again come forth
into the plain. In this manner we give time for the
arrival of reinforcements from England, your army to

be formed and equipped, and that of the South to
come forth. In short, the game of Spain and of
England, which must always be the same, is to
procrastinate and to gain time; and not, if it can be
helped, to place the whole stake upon the hazard of a
battle.'

Sir John, having spelled out his reasons for retreat, finished
by excusing the misconduct of his men on the surliness of the
Spaniards themselves:

'The people of this part of Spain seem to be less well-
disposed than those I have hitherto met with. They
perhaps think that we mean to abandon them. It would
have a good effect if you explained to them, in a
proclamation, that this was by no means either your
intention or that of the British army; and call upon the
Alcaldes and *Corregidors*[3] to remain at their posts, and to
be of all the use in their power to the different armies
both Spanish and British. Some of them of late have
run away from the towns; which has been the
unavoidable cause of irregularities having been
committed by the troops; for, when the magistrates are
not present to give regularly, the soldier must take, and
this produces a mischievous habit.'

There were some, however, even within Moore's inner
circle, who blamed the general himself for the breakdown in
discipline. August Schaumann, a German civilian serving as a
deputy assistant commissary-general,[4] perhaps spoke for many
when he wrote:

'At the very beginning of the retrograde movement,
disorder, a lack of discipline and subordination must
have set in, and this was brought about in the first
place through the rapid marches, secondly through
deficient victuals, appalling weather and bad roads,
and finally through the dejection and sense of
ignominy caused by a continuous retreat and the
inability to measure oneself with the enemy,
complicated by the fact that General Moore
maintained throughout, the most absolute secrecy and

silence regarding the movement. He was very much
blamed for this, for it was the wrong time for secrecy,
and he ought to have acquainted all officers and men
with the necessity for the retreat long before. Even the
officers became careless; and no one knew the why or
whither of all that was happening. The only thing that
everybody believed was that all must now be lost.'

Indeed it must have appeared so to the sodden, footsore
infantry, as Moore, realising that the line of the Esla could not
be held, announced his intention to push on to Astorga, via
La Baneza, as soon as possible. Hope and Fraser would march
the following day, 28 December, and the Reserve, Light
Brigades and cavalry, twenty-four hours later. Baird,
meanwhile, was ordered to decamp from Valencia and head
for Astorga forthwith. As for Romana, Napier informs us that:

'Sir John requested him to maintain Leon as long as
possible and leave Galicia open for the English army.
Romana assented to both requests, and as he had a
great rabble, and a number of citizens and volunteers
were willing and even eager to fight, the town might
have made resistance. Moore hoped it would, and gave
orders to break down the bridge at Castrogonzalo in
his own front, the moment the stragglers and baggage
should have passed.'

For the time being, however, the army was to enjoy a
much-needed day of rest. Schaumann, who, upon his arrival
at Benavente had found it to be 'extremely picturesque' and
'full of the most wonderful things', took the opportunity to do
some sightseeing. Intrigued by the romantic aspect of a
Moorish-Gothic castle – the ancestral home of the Duchess of
Ossuna who, on the approach of the French had fled to Seville
– Schaumann resolved to satisfy his curiosity:

'There were two regiments of infantry, together with
three batteries of artillery, quartered in the apartments
of this magnificent ancient building, where, in the old
days, none but proud knights, barons and bannerets
aired their armour, and quaffed golden goblets to the

accompaniment of songs and string music; and the soldiers were carrying on their noisy life, vouchsafing the relics and artistic treasures that surrounded them neither attention nor admiration. What the English soldier cannot see any purpose in does not interest him. Everywhere bayonets and nails were stuck into the crevices of precious columns, or into the beautifully decorated walls, and knapsacks and cartridge boxes were hung upon them. In the large fireplaces, decorated with marble, there burned huge fires, kept alive with broken pieces of antique furniture, either gilt or artistically carved; and the same thing was going on in the courtyard, where the walls were all black with smoke. On these fires stood a number of camp kettles. The soldiers' wives were washing their things and hanging them just where they chose. A good deal was wantonly destroyed, and every corner was scoured for hidden treasure. The English soldier, who was now quite well aware that he had been lured into this country and into a parlous position by the Spaniards under false pretences, and had been left in the lurch; also that he only had the choice of flying in ignominious retreat before an enemy thrice as strong as his own army in numbers and in whose defeat he had come to assist, or else of being uselessly sacrificed through treachery, set about burning everything out of revenge. It was a good thing, though, that he wreaked his vengeance only on inanimate objects, and not on the inhabitants of the country. The officers, who were residing in various parts of the castle, enraged by their men's lust of destruction and desecration, seemed crushed with grief, and did all in their power to limit the damage as far as possible; but the numbers were too much for them and the hidden corners too numerous. They could not be everywhere. Besides, insubordination was already apparent among the men, and in spite of all the discipline, it was impossible to stop it in an army which already felt that it was retreating from a country it hated.'

Meanwhile, three miles away on the banks of the Esla, Craufurd's Light Brigade was posted on the hostile shore, guarding the approaches to Castrogonzalo and its vital bridge. At 5.00 p. m. the cavalry arrived from Valderas; and while the 3rd Hussars of the King's German Legion[5] were detailed to picket the bridge, Paget's remaining regiments trotted over it and on to Benavente. It was now that, according to Napier:

> 'Craufurd commenced destroying the bridge amidst torrents of rain and snow; half the troops worked, the other half kept the enemy at bay from the heights on the left bank, for the cavalry scouts of the Imperial Guard were spread over the plain.'

Demolishing the sturdy bridge, however, was to be no easy matter, as noted by Ensign Robert Blakeney of the 28th Regiment:

> 'The bridge being constructed of such solid material, the greatest exertions were required to penetrate the masonry; and from the hurried manner and sudden necessity of the march from Sahagun, there had been no time to send an engineer forward to prepare for the undertaking. These circumstances much retarded the work, and an incessant fall of heavy rain and sleet rendered the whole operation excessively laborious and fatiguing.'

At 10.00 p. m. the French mounted a series of attacks on Craufurd's outposts and some hot skirmishing ensued. Benjamin Harris, whose battalion was stationed about a mile from the bridge, at the village of Castro Pipa, describes how:

> 'Behind broken-down carts and tumbrils, huge trunks of trees and everything we could scrape together, the Rifles lay and blazed away at the advancing cavalry,'

while the poor villagers were,

> '. . . aroused from their beds to behold their village almost on fire with our continued discharges. They ran from their houses crying, "*Viva l'Englisa!*" and "*Viva la*

Franca!" [*sic*] in one breath and flew to the open country in alarm.'

Next morning, amidst a storm of rain and sleet, Lefebvre-Desnouëttes continued to launch further assaults against the bridgehead – all of which were foiled – and eventually the skirmishing slackened into an uneasy stand-off, with the British, in Harris' words, 'standing for many hours with arms posted and staring the French cavalry in the face, while the water actually ran out of the muzzles of their muskets.' Meanwhile, the agonisingly slow demolition work on the bridge continued.

With the fall of dusk, the hussars of the German Legion were withdrawn from the perimeter and pulled back over the bridge, prior to its destruction. Twenty troopers remained on picket duty at the water's edge, while the remainder of the regiment were ordered to rest. Major von Linsingen, however, fearing the French might ford the river under cover of darkness, kept his horses saddled and his men on the alert for the remainder of the wild and stormy night.

At midnight, according to Robert Blakeney:

> '. . . the preparations at the bridge being completed, the troops retired. Fortunately it was dark, rainy and tempestuous; and so the Light Brigade passed unobserved over the bridge to the friendly side in profound silence, except for the roaring of the waters and the tempest, and without the slightest opposition. Immediately on our gaining the right bank the mine was sprung with full effect, blowing up two arches, together with the buttress by which they had been supported.'

Benjamin Harris, one of the last to cross the bridge, was felled by the blast as the charges were detonated:

> 'The Staff Corps had been hard at work mining the centre of the structure, which was filled with gunpowder, so we had to pass over by means of a narrow plank. All was nearly up with me. I felt that it

would be all I could accomplish to reach the end of the plank but we all got to the other side safely. Almost immediately the bridge blew up. It was a tremendous report, and a house at its extremity burst into flames. My limbs were already tremulous so the concussion of the explosion threw me to the ground where, almost insensible, I lay flat on my face for some time. After a while I recovered but it was only with extreme difficulty and after many more falls that I succeeded in regaining the column and reached Benavente.'

When Craufurd's Brigade entered Benavente, they were, according to Blakeney, 'so excessively fatigued, having worked incessantly and laboured severely for nearly two days and two nights, their clothes drenched through the whole time, that they could scarcely keep their eyes open.' Sadly, the reception they received from the townsfolk was as indifferent as the weather. Given the deplorable conduct of the first British troops to enter Benavente this was, perhaps, only to be expected. Furthermore, many Spaniards were only too conscious of the fact that the British were abandoning them, and that in their wake would come French occupation and reprisals.

Under such circumstances, Robert Blakeney was no doubt making an understatement, when he wrote of a 'want of good feeling towards the British,' and the following anecdote – quoted from Blakeney's memoirs – affords a good example of a typical *impasse*:

'After the destruction of the Gonzolo bridge, when the 52nd Regiment marched into Benavente, though benumbed with wet and cold, yet they could not procure a single pint of wine for the men, either for love or money, or for mere humanity which under such circumstances would have moved the breast of most men to an act of charitable generosity. During the anxious pleading to the feelings and the dogged denial, a sergeant of his company came to Lieutenant Love of the above-mentioned regiment, informing him that in an outhouse belonging to the convent in which they were billeted he discovered a wall recently built up, by which he conjectured that some wine might have been concealed. Love instantly waited on the friars, whom he entreated to let the men have some wine, at the same time offering prompt payment. The holy fat father abbot constantly declared, by a long catalogue of saints, that there was not a drop in the convent. Love, although a very young man at the time, was not easily imposed upon. Reconnoitring the premises, he had a rope tied round his body, and in this manner got himself lowered through a sort of skylight down into the outhouse, where the sergeant had discovered the fresh masonry through a crevice in the strongly barricaded door. After his landing, the rope was drawn up, and two men of the company followed in the same manner. They fortunately found a log of wood, which, aided by the ropes, they converted into a battering ram, and four or five strong percussions well directed breached the newly built wall. Now rushing through the breach, they found the inner chamber to be the very sanctorum of Bacchus. Wine sufficient was found to give every man in the company a generous allowance. The racy juice was contained in a large vat, and while they were issuing it out in perfect order to the drenched and shivering soldiers, the fat prior suddenly made his appearance through a trap-door and laughingly requested that at least he might have one drink before all was consumed. Upon this one of the men remarked, "By Jove! When the wine was his, he was damned stingy about it; but now that it is ours, we will show him what British hospitality is and give him his fill!" So saying, he seized the holy fat man and chucked him head foremost into the vat; and had it not been for Love and some other officers, who by this time had found their way into the cellar, the Franciscan worshipper of Bacchus would most probably have shared the fate of George Duke of Clarence, except that the wine was not Malmsey. . . '

That night, the 2nd and 3rd Divisions marched out of
Benavente, *en route* for Astorga and the rendezvous with Baird,
some forty miles to the north-west. There had been insufficient
time to distribute all the army's stores, and insufficient
transport to remove what was left. The troops, therefore, were
told to grab what they could from the piles of food and
clothing, which lay by the roadside as they filed out of town.
Whatever remained would be consigned to the flames.

And so Moore had won 'the race for Benavente' and
thwarted the Emperor. Added to this *coup*, the road to Astorga
– the gateway to the Galicias – remained open, his hussars had
bloodied their French opponents at every turn, and Craufurd's
demolition of the Castrogonzalo bridge had been so complete
that Napoleon would be kept at bay for a further twenty-four
hours. A high price had been paid, however, for these assets:
his soldiers' morale was fast ebbing, their discipline cracking,
while relations with the Spaniards had degenerated into open
hostility. Although most of Moore's troops believed they would
fight a major battle before reaching the mountains, Sir John's
eyes were already searching for the sea; and before preparing
to quit Benavente with the Reserve, he set down the following
lines to Castlereagh in London:

> 'The roads are very bad, and the means of carriage
> scanty. If I am pressed . . . I may be forced to fight a
> battle. This, however, I shall endeavour to avoid, for
> certainly in the present state of things, it is more
> Buonaparte's game than mine. It is said he comes
> himself, with 10,000 of his Guards. The force moving
> against us cannot be less than 50,000 – we should,
> when at Astorga, be about 27,000 . . . The country
> about Astorga offers no advantage to an inferior army.
> I shall, therefore, not stop there longer than to secure
> the stores, and shall retreat to Villafranca, where I
> understand there is a position. But if the French press
> me, I must hasten to the coast.'

Notes

1. Londonderry, Marquess of, *Story of the Peninsular War.*
2. The 1st Duke of Wellington, quoted in Haythornthwaite, *Who was Who in the Napoleonic Wars.*
3. The titles of *Alcalde* and *Corregidor* translate as Mayor and Chief Magistrate, respectively.
4. The Commissariat was a civilian outfit run by the Treasury, with the specific task of obtaining the army's daily rations. Assistant Commissaries, their Deputies and clerks, were attached to infantry brigades and cavalry regiments: their superiors were the Commissary-General and his Assistant and Deputies.
5. A dynastic possession of the German-bred British royal family, Hanover provided some of the British Army's best troops of the period. The King's German Legion was formed in 1803 from exiled Hanoverians loyal to George III, and its performance – especially that of the cavalry – was marked by a high degree of professionalism.

CHAPTER 4

Vivan Los Ingleses!

At daybreak on 29 December, the Reserve Division and Light Brigades followed in the footsteps of the vanguard and struck the road north for La Baneza and Astorga. Behind them, Benavente presented a sorry sight. Its streets were choked with wreckage and debris dumped by the retreating soldiers and the Castle of Ossuna – trashed, set afire and gutted the previous evening – was left a sad, smouldering ruin. The only British personnel left in town were Sir John, his staff, the clerks of the Commissariat (busy disposing of the remaining stores), and Lord Paget's cavalry, whose pickets still guarded the broken bridge at Castrogonzalo.

Napoleon, however, was now hurrying to the scene from Valderas, furious at the hold-up on the banks of the Esla. Having lost 'the race for Benavente', he now feared that the 'English' (Napoleon habitually used this term in preference to 'British') might flee before he brought them to battle and simply melt away into the mountains of Galicia. He urged General Lefebvre-Desnouëttes, therefore, to cross the river with the cavalry of the Imperial Guard, maintain contact with Moore, and discover which route his redcoats had taken. Lefebvre had observed the British infantry file out of Benavente at first light and, gazing across the river in the chill morning air, could now see nothing to oppose his passage but a puny picket of hussars. Consequently, when a suitable ford was discovered a few hundred yards from the demolished bridge, the French general put himself at the head of 600 horsemen of the Chasseurs à Cheval[1] of the Imperial Guard and led them into the ice-cold water, as Lord Paget was soon told:

> 'About nine o'clock I received a report that the enemy's cavalry was in the act of crossing the river at the ford near the bridge. I immediately sent down the pickets of the night under Lieutenant-Colonel Otway of the 18th, having left orders that the cavalry should repair to their alarm posts.'

Otway, joined by Major Burgwedel[2] of the 3rd German Hussars, commanded a body of about 200 men, but they could not form up in time to prevent the French from emerging onto dry land and deploying in battle order. Thus, outnumbered three-to-one, Otway's hussars – despite fierce fighting and prodigies of valour – were propelled backwards by an unstoppable mass of men and horses. Meanwhile, in the words of William Napier:

> '...the plain was covered with stragglers, baggage-mules and followers of the army, the town was filled with tumult, the distant pickets and *vedettes* were seen galloping in from the right and left, the French were pressing forward boldly, and every appearance indicated that the enemy's whole army was come up and passing the river.'

As Otway was jostled into Benavente's suburbs, he was joined by about sixty troopers from the inlying picket, under Major Quentin, plus twenty-five men of the 18th Hussars. Otway halted his combined force astride the main road, its flanks covered by garden walls, and as the French came on, ordered a charge. The British horsemen crashed into the leading French squadrons but broke once again on a solid wall of supports. It was at this moment that Lord Paget – 'twirling his moustachios' – arrived on the scene, accompanied by General Stewart with the remainder of the 3rd German Hussars. Paget, who immediately saw the possibility of hitting

Lefebvre's *chasseurs* in their exposed left flank, dashed back into town to collect the 10th and the remainder of the 18th Hussars from their billets, leaving Stewart to buy time with yet another charge. Led this time by Quentin, the assault was again rebuffed by sheer weight of numbers and the hard-pressed hussars were pushed back to the very gates of Benavente. They were now trapped, and as Lefebvre's 'Invincibles' advanced to deliver the *coup de grâce*, Stewart's men prepared to sell their lives dearly.

At that moment, having approached unseen through the suburbs, Paget appeared on Lefebvre's left with 450 men of the 10th Hussars supported by 200 of the 18th. The tables were now turned and, before the French could react, Paget's supports slammed into their flank with devastating effect: 'One cheer was given,' recalled Stewart, 'and the horses being pressed to their speed, the enemy's line was broken in an instant.'

The French squadrons now made a three-mile dash for the Esla, the British in hot pursuit, sabreing the stragglers. Meanwhile, the good folk of Benavente – who had lined the city walls to watch the drama unfolding beneath – burst into wild cheers of '*Vivan los Ingleses!*'

The French veterans were pursued to the very water's edge. Those riders who could not urge their horses into the swollen river were hacked down or taken prisoner, while those whose mounts floundered midstream were popped at with pistols and carbines. Most, however, made the apparent safety of the opposite bank and formed up as if to continue the fight, but the arrival of Dowman's Troop of horse artillery, firing 'Colonel Shrapnel's shells', soon put them to flight. Stewart described the results of the action:

> 'This was ... the most serious affair in which we had as yet been engaged. The cavalry opposed to us formed part of the Imperial Guard; they were tried soldiers and fought in a manner not unworthy of the reputation which they had earned in the north of Europe. They lost in killed and wounded, independently of prisoners, about sixty men, while our casualties fell somewhat

short of fifty ... It was said that Napoleon himself was an eyewitness of this *rencontre*,[3] from the opposite heights. Whether there be any truth in the report, I know not; but one thing is certain, that the enemy did not venture, for some days after, to oppose themselves hand-to-hand with our cavalry.'

This was, perhaps, hardly surprising, considering the frightful carnage doled out that morning; though fatalities had been fairly light – fifty-five Frenchmen killed and fifty British (almost all from the pickets which had borne the initial brunt of the fighting) – the wounds sustained by both sides were truly horrific. According to John Mollo, in his excellent study of the British hussars in Spain, *The Prince's Dolls*:

> 'French heads and arms were lopped off wholesale, while many of the British were badly cut about the head, because their tall fur caps had no chin-straps and fell off at the first blow.'

Baron Larrey, chief surgeon to the Imperial Guard, later claimed to have treated over seventy men for sabre cuts to the head alone. 'The clashing of the swords were [*sic*] similar to a number of mowers whetting their scythes,' recorded one onlooker; while August Schaumann of the Commissariat testified that:

> 'The sword work during this cavalry *mêlée* is said to have been terrible, and our Germans are believed to have been mad with rage. Most of the enemy's wounded had their arms cut off, and in many cases their upper limbs hung from their shoulders merely by a shred of their uniforms. Lieutenant, now Major, Heise, told me about many of the heavier blows that had brought men down. He saw one Frenchman lying on the ground who had had the whole of his head cut off horizontally above the eyes at one blow, and many others with heads split in two. He also noticed one man who rode by with outstretched arms who had received a diagonal blow across his face which had cut his mouth right open so that his jaw, as far back as the tongue, hung

down over his chest, and you could see his gullet. One of our hussars had had his head cut off, and many of our fellows pursued the enemy right into the middle of the stream and brought back prisoners.'

These captives – 'powerful looking fellows' according to Schaumann – numbered some seventy-two men and included Poles, Italians, Swiss, and Germans.[4] They were, Schaumann informs us:

> '...collected together in one house ...A crowd of Spaniards are standing before the door, and bitterly regret that they are prevented by the English sentries from murdering the prisoners on the spot. Many of them are Germans just come across the Pyrenees ...and they remarked jokingly that the Emperor was waging war on their legs.'

One prisoner, however, was singled out for special treatment, for he was none other than General Charles Lefebvre-Desnouëttes himself. Captured during the flight to the ford, Lefebvre was led back to Benavente, blood pouring from a gash in his forehead,[5] smiling forlornly at the flocks of gawping onlookers.

The son of a draper who had enlisted as a simple dragoon in 1793, Lefebvre had risen to become a general of division, colonel of Napoleon's escort – the Chasseurs à Cheval of the Imperial Guard – and a count of the Empire. He was a personal favourite of the Emperor's and had married Napoleon's second cousin. His capture, therefore, was a major triumph for Moore, who personally tended the general's wound, gave him clean linen from his own wardrobe and fed him tea and toast, while the Spaniards outside howled for his blood.

Within hours, Lefebvre's luggage arrived under a flag of truce, and that evening he dined at Moore's table, resplendent in his *chasseur*'s full-dress uniform. Sir John, noticing that Lefebvre was without a sword and his *ensemble*, therefore, incomplete, offered him a fine East India blade of his own. Polite but glum, the Frenchman sat through the meal, repeatedly observing that Napoleon, 'never forgave the unfortunate.' Moore, anxious to avoid upsetting his 'guest' further, thought better of asking him to sign a paper promising not to escape.[6]

While the British relished the propaganda *coup* afforded by Lefebvre's capture, considerable controversy raged over who had actually bagged him. The officers of the 3rd German Hussars asserted that the hero was one of their own, a certain Johann Bergmann, who had been simple enough to entrust his prize to an English soldier, while he carried on fighting, and a sworn statement was produced to support the claim. Meanwhile, a soldier of the 7th Hussars, who had delivered up Lefebvre's watch to a senior officer, was also reputed to have been involved in the capture.

The laurels, however, eventually went to one Levi Grisdale, a private in the 10th Hussars, who apparently took the French general prisoner on the banks of the Esla, when his wounded horse refused to enter the water. Grisdale was later rewarded by the Prince of Wales for his feat, being promoted to corporal, and – having become something of a celebrity – eventually opened a pub in Penrith, called 'The General Lefebvre'.

Interestingly, although Napoleon was mortified by the loss of Lefebvre-Desnouëttes and the defeat of his 'Invincibles', the effect upon the French army as a whole was quite the reverse, for, according to General Sarrazin:

> '. . . every regiment, without exception, was delighted to hear that the English had lowered the pride of those *chasseurs*; for there was not a man who did not fancy himself a hero, after the success which this corps had obtained against the Russian imperial guard at the battle of Austerlitz.'

Paget's hussar-heroes quit Benavente on the evening of the 29th, leaving the men of the Commissariat to complete their work of destruction. Casks of rum were emptied into the gutters; and in the gardens of a monastery (which had served as Moore's main depot), bonfires were made of forsaken heaps of army kit and foodstuffs. Determined not to leave anything of value to the French, the Commissariat invited the townsfolk to join in the final liquidation of the army's stores and the incredulous Spaniards – delirious at the prospect of obtaining a year's supply of food and clothing overnight – fell into a frenzy which would continue late into the night. Deputy Assistant Commissary-General August Schaumann recorded the scene:

'All the inhabitants of the town rushed to the spot and were regularly invited to snatch what they could and what an orgy it was for the Spaniards, who are so good at snatching! I, too, was not idle, and laying a number of the finest blankets and a quantity of biscuits and rum aside, fetched my landlord and made him take the whole lot to his house.'

Captain Gordon, before vacating town with the 15th Hussars, noted that:

'...immense magazines of stores of every description were burned, and several thousand pairs of shoes were destroyed or given to the Spaniards, at the very time when a great portion of our infantry was but ill-provided with that article of equipment.'

Meanwhile, on the road to La Baneza, the scales at last fell from the eyes of the footsore infantry, and the reality of their situation became apparent to Benjamin Harris and his comrades at least:

'The discovery was made to our company by a good-tempered, jolly fellow, named Patrick McLauchlan. He inquired of our destination of an officer, marching directly in his front: "By Jesus, Musther Hills," I heard him say, "where the devil is this you're taking us?" "To England, McLauchlan," returned the officer, a melancholy smile upon his face, "if we can get there." The information McLauchlan had obtained from Lieutenant Hill quickly spread amongst us, and we saw more clearly the horrors of our situation. The men murmured at not being permitted to turn and stand at bay. They cursed the French and swore they would rather die 10,000 deaths with their rifles in their hands in opposition, than endure the present toil.'

For toil it was, and though the leading columns had reached Astorga the previous day, Private Harris and his comrades of the 95th came across many who – from exhaustion or intoxication – had quit their colours and dropped out on the road. William Surtees also witnessed similar scenes:

> 'A most lamentable number of stragglers were overtaken by us ... they had either fallen out from excessive fatigue, or from having (as in too many instances) drunk too much; indeed, the destruction of the magazine of provisions at the place we had left, enabled too many of them to obtain by one means or other considerable quantities of spirits, and which, of course, rendered them incapable of marching. This was a long and wearisome day's journey of nearly thirty miles; we did not reach La Baneza till late at night, where a considerable quantity of ammunition was obliged to be destroyed, the animals failing which drew it.'

As midnight struck in Benavente, Commissary Schaumann noted that:

> '... the tumult in the stores depot reached its zenith and no one any longer felt safe. The bulk of the army, headquarters and everybody had gone, and the French, who were at the gates of the town were, according to all accounts, expected to enter at any moment, or at the very latest, early the following morning. While, therefore, the whole crowd were amusing themselves, eating, drinking, raving, shouting, quarrelling and destroying, I took a last piece of salt meat, a handkerchief full of barley, some biscuits, a pair of boots, and three woollen blankets, and creeping out softly, like a fox from a dovecot, reached home at 1.00 a. m. I then fed my horse, made my amiable host a present of everything I had taken from the stores,

and lay down to rest a bit, but scarcely had the dawn
broken when I galloped out of Benavente and away.'

Schaumann escaped in the nick of time. Thousands of
French cavalry were at that moment crossing the ford at
Castrogonzalo and, finding no British, spilling onto the plain
beyond.

Notes

1. Sources vary in their description of Lefebvre's force: some
   state that four squadrons of *chasseurs à cheval* made the
   crossing, others that it was three squadrons of *chasseurs* plus a
   mixed squadron of Mamelukes and *chevaux-légers*. At any rate,
   most sources agree that 550–600 Imperial troops were
   deployed.
2. Burgwedel would be the only officer hurt in the action from
   the British side.
3. Captain Gordon recorded in his journal that, 'It was known
   that Bonaparte slept at Villalpando, which is only five
   leagues from Benavente, on 28 December and it may be
   presumed that he suffered a severe mortification at the
   defeat sustained by the Hussars of his Guard, almost within
   his own view.'
4. This mix of nationalities were apparently all *chasseurs à cheval*,
   being dressed – according to Schaumann – in the imperial
   uniform of 'large bearskin busbies' and 'dark green
   uniforms'. William Surtees describes them as, 'fine-looking
   men, dressed in dark-green long coats with high bear-skin
   caps and moustaches, which gave them a formidable
   appearance.'
5. All sources agree that General Lefebvre-Desnouëttes was
   captured when his horse refused to enter the river, but there
   is some confusion as to precisely what happened next: some
   reports say that he was wounded by a pistol ball, others that
   he received a sabre cut, others do not mention a wound at
   all.
6. Lefebvre-Desnouëttes was sent to England and lived on
   parole at Cheltenham, where his charm and good looks
   made him something of a local dignitary. He was joined by
   his wife in 1812 and, with her aid, broke parole and made

good his escape to France, disguised as a Russian nobleman. Napoleon welcomed his favourite back with open arms, restoring him to a command in time for the Russian invasion of June 1812.

Abandoned By Everything Spanish

'The English are running away as fast they can!' declared a triumphant Napoleon as he entered Benavente on the morning of 30 December. Yet, as Sir Charles Oman, points out:

> 'All that the rapid forced marches of the Emperor had brought him was the privilege of assisting at Paget's departure, and of picking up in Benavente some abandoned carts, which Moore had caused to be broken after burning their contents.'

In fact, Napoleon's troops were suffering, just as much as Moore's, from lack of food and sleep, foul weather, and endless marching over miserable roads. Desperate to catch Moore at all costs, Napoleon had driven his men so hard that some, unable to take further punishment, resorted to suicide. Georges Blond, in his study of Napoleon's military machine, *La Grande Armeé*, states that, on 28 December, twelve soldiers of the Guard took their own lives, while the French columns 'resembled a funeral *cortège*, strung out over dozens of leagues.' The Emperor, however, remained ebullient: Marshal Soult, the Duke of Dalmatia, would catch the 'English' at Astorga, and the pains of his soldiers would be recompensed.

But the Duke of Dalmatia (dubbed 'the Duke of Damnation' by the British) was only just nearing Mansilla, heavy weather and bad roads having delayed him to such a degree that he had barely covered forty-five miles in three days. As already noted, Romana had left the vital bridge at Mansilla complete, guarded by 3,000 men broken in spirit, while he himself occupied the nearby city of Leon. A serious enough error in itself,[1] Romana's commander on the spot, General Martinengo,[2] compounded it by placing his troops in front of the bridge with the river to their backs. Thus, when the 2,200 sabres of Soult's cavalry[3] arrived, a single charge was all that was needed to raise a storm of panic among the Spaniards. In writing of this action, Oman states that, 'pursuers and pursued went pell-mell over the bridge, which was not defended for a moment.' In the event, hundreds of Spaniards were herded into the river and butchered like cattle, 1,500 were taken prisoner, and the remainder fled in terror.

When Romana learned of the disaster at Mansilla, he immediately decamped, leaving Leon to Soult, who took possession of the city and its stores the following day, without firing a shot. This was a bitter blow for Moore, who had counted upon a show of resistance, especially as Leon formed a bulwark on his northern flank. Now he was vulnerable to attacks and outflanking manoeuvres from both Soult in the north and Napoleon in the south. Thus it seemed that Sir John was destined to be, in the words of brother James, 'perpetually disappointed in every assistance that was expected from the Spaniards.'

Romana had not done with creating calamities. For, as James Moore recorded, instead of retiring north into the Asturias, leaving Astorga and its resources to Moore as agreed, he made straight for the latter place, obstructing the British line of march and filling the town with 10,000 sick and starving troops:

> 'Thus the Spanish army, instead of being of the slightest
> utility to the English, by consuming the provisions, and

filling the roads with their mules and carts, were a most serious impediment.'

This interruption was a catastrophe for Sir John, who had planned to feed and refit his men from Astorga's well-stocked magazines; but Romana's troops were even more destitute than his own, and as Napier records:

'. . . when the English divisions marched in, such a tumult and confusion arose, that no distribution could be made nor the destruction of the stores effected.'

A walled town, standing in the shadow of the Galician Mountains, Astorga was a major military depot, and the British troops believed that here, at last, Moore would stand and fight. But, as the redcoats entered the settlement between 29 and 31 December, they discovered not a haven, but the very picture of hell. Dead bodies – primarily victims of typhus – lay unburied in the narrow streets; wounded men languished untended in carts or on filthy floors; and every building was crammed with sick, starving, shivering, Spanish soldiers. A cold, clammy fog completed this macabre tableau, which was accompanied by the pitiful wailing of the town's waifs and womenfolk. The 'Soldier of the 71st' was dismayed by what he saw:

'We reached Astorga, which we were led to believe was to be our resting-place, and the end of our fatigues. Here we found the army of General Romana. I can convey no description of it in words. It had more the appearance of a large body of peasants, driven from their homes, famished and in want of everything, than a regular army. Sickness was making dreadful havoc amongst them.'

The condition of Romana's men – the remnants of the Army of Galicia – so shocked the incoming British, that many were overcome with a sense of pity, mingled with horror: 'It is hardly possible to conceive men bearing less resemblance to soldiers or having a stronger claim upon compassion, than these wretched creatures,' wrote General Charles Stewart; while Captain Gordon observed that the Spaniards were:

> '. . . all ill-clothed; many were without shoes, and even without arms; a pestilential fever raged amongst them; they had been without bread for several days, and were quite destitute of money . . . I spoke to some of the men, who were evidently suffering from famine and disease; they declared they had eaten nothing for three days, and when we gave them the remains of our dinner and money to buy wine, their expressions of gratitude were unbounded.'

Robert Blakeney of the 28th Regiment, however, noted that it was not only the Spaniards who were troublesome:

> 'The Spaniards, shivering from partial nakedness and voracious from continued hunger, committed the greatest disorders in search of food and raiment . . . their bad example was eagerly followed by the British soldiers in their insatiable thirst for wine. . . '

Denied the food and shelter they had been promised – most of which had been appropriated by Astorga's townsfolk – many British soldiers took to prowling the streets in search of alcohol. When they finally discovered the wine cellars, a debauch of drunken delinquency quickly followed. Fights were started with Romana's troops over possession of the best billets; shops and houses were looted; and when Spanish artillery officers attempted to stop the redcoats from stealing their mules, they were bluntly told to 'mind their own bloody business'. The excesses committed by the British moved Romana to lodge an official complaint with Moore, but as many regimental officers had simply given up trying to control their men, these lamentations had little effect.

Meanwhile, despite a near-riot by needy British infantrymen, valuable stores which had survived the rapacity of the Spaniards were destroyed by the over-zealous jobsworths of the Commissariat. These included thousands of pairs of shoes, even though many soldiers were now limping about barefoot, their boots having simply disintegrated.

William Surtees describes one such scene of official profligacy, involving the soldiers' beloved rum:

> 'The . . . casks were ordered to be staved, and to let the contents run out on the street, that they might not fall into the hands of the enemy: thus the rum which had cost so much trouble in bringing up all the way from Corunna was about to be lost forever; a thing most heart-rending to the numerous soldiers looking on, who loved it so dearly. However, they were determined not to lose all, for when the heads of the casks were knocked in, and their contents permitted to run in streams down the gutters, some of those brutes deliberately took off their greasy caps, and laving up the rum and the mud together, drank, or rather ate, the swinish mixture.'

The men of the Reserve Division entered town on 30 December in search of a good meal and, as Blakeney recounts, some eschewed brute force in favour of cunning, in order to obtain one:

> 'It was on that night which we passed at Astorga that I discovered a circumstance of which I had not been previously aware: namely, that in the Light Company of the 28th Regiment, there was a complete and well-organised band of ventriloquists, who could imitate any species of bird or animal so perfectly, that it was scarcely possible to discover the difference between the imitation and the natural tone of the animal imitated. Soon after we contrived to get into some kind of quarter, the men being in the same apartment with the officers owing to the crowd and confusion, a soldier named Savage, immediately on entering the room, began to crow like a cock, and then placed his ear close to the keyhole of a door leading into another apartment which was locked. After remaining in this attentive position for some moments, he removed to another part of the room and repeated his crowing. I began to think that the man was drunk or insane, never before having perceived in him the slightest want

of proper respect for his superiors. Upon my asking him what he meant by such extraordinary conduct in the presence of officers, he with a smile replied, "I believe we have them, sir." This seemingly unconnected reply confirmed me in the opinion I had formed of his mental derangement, the more particularly as his incoherent reply was instantly followed by another crow; this was answered apparently in the same voice, but somewhat fainter. Savage then jumped up, crying out, "Here they are!" and insisted upon having the door opened; and when this was reluctantly done by the inhabitants of the house, a fine cock followed by many hens came strutting into the room with all the pomp of a sultan attended by his many queens. The head of the polygamist, together with those of his superfluous wives, was soon severed from his body, notwithstanding the loud remonstrances of the former owners who, failing in their entreaties that the harem should be spared, demanded remuneration; but whether the men paid for what they had taken like grovelling citizens, or offered political reasons as an apology like great monarchs, I now cannot call to mind. But however the affair may have been arranged, the act was venial, for had the fowls been spared by our men they must have fallen into the stomachs of our enemies next day; and it is not one of the least important duties of a retreating army to carry away or destroy anything which may be useful to their pursuers, however severely the inhabitants may suffer.'

Moore also arrived on the 30th and, as at Benavente, was dismayed by the scenes of disorder and indiscipline which were all too apparent. A humanitarian, who preferred to motivate men via *esprit de corps*, rather than the lash, Sir John made an urgent appeal to the stoicism of his soldiers, the honour of his officers, and the bravery of all:

'The present is a moment when the army is necessarily called upon to make great efforts, and to submit to privations, the bearing cheerfully with which is a

quality not less estimable than valour ... The goodwill
of the inhabitants will be particularly useful to the
army, and can only be obtained by good conduct on
the part of the troops ... The Commander of the
Forces cannot impress too strongly on the whole army
the necessity of this; and he trusts that the generals and
the commanding officers will adopt such measures,
both on the march and in cantonments, as will ensure
it ... It is very probable that the army will shortly have
to meet with the enemy; and the Commander of the
Forces has no doubt that they will eagerly imitate the
worthy example which has been set them by the
cavalry, on several recent occasions, and particularly in
the affair of yesterday; in which Brigadier-General
Stewart, with an inferior force, charged and overthrew
one of the best corps of cavalry in the French army
... The generals will immediately inspect the baggage
of the brigades and divisions. They are held responsible
that it does not exceed the proportion fixed by the
General Orders.'

Moore had previously let it be known that he hoped to
make a stand at Astorga and, upon his arrival, Romana tried
to persuade him to hold the mountain passes of Foncebadon
and Manzanal, in the rear of the town. The idea was not
totally without merit. Astorga still contained some stores of
food; fresh muskets and ammunition had recently arrived from
Corunna; and 25,000 British troops were more than enough to
defend the two narrow defiles – yet Sir John dismissed the
possibility out of hand. He had achieved his goal of drawing
the French away from the unconquered south, and saw no
reason to take further risks for a people who, in his opinion,
would not help him and *could not* help themselves. He wrote in
this vein to Castlereagh:

'Abandoned from the beginning by everything Spanish,
we were equal to nothing by ourselves. From a desire
to do what I could, I made the movement against
Soult. As a diversion it has answered completely: but
as there is nothing to take advantage of it, I have risked

the loss of an army to no purpose. I find no option now but to fall down to the coast as fast as I am able ... The army would, there cannot be a doubt, have distinguished itself, had the Spaniards been able to offer any resistance. But from the first it was placed in situations in which, without the possibility of doing any good, it was itself constantly risked.'

Moore's soldiers, however, would have welcomed risk, if it meant closing with the enemy, and regarded any further retrograde movement as 'a shameless flight'. Matters were not helped by the fact that a number of Sir John's own generals were openly criticising his policy to their inferiors, the common view being that their commander's duty was to lead them into battle, not away from it. Consequently, the retreat from Astorga constituted a body-blow to British morale, although the visible effects varied from regiment to regiment, depending upon the quality and experience of the officers and NCOs. By all accounts, the cavalry, artillery, German Legion, and Foot Guards, maintained high levels of discipline, as did the 20th, 43rd, 52nd, and 95th Regiments. Many other units, however, simply fell apart, as noted by Charles Stewart:

> 'In Astorga, the blowing up of ammunition wagons, the destruction of entrenching tools and the committal of field equipments to the flames for a whole division, gave signal for all the bad passions of those who witnessed them, to let loose; and, mortifying as it is to confess it, the fact cannot be denied, that from that hour we no longer resembled a British army.'

Moore did not linger at Astorga, his most pressing need being to reach the mountains ahead of his pursuers, in order to avoid encirclement. In fact, the divisions under Hope, Fraser, and Baird, which constituted Moore's vanguard, were ordered out of town and on to Villafranca, via Bembibre, on the very day of his arrival. The 'Private of the 42nd' was marching with Baird's 1st Division:

> 'I shudder as I reflect on the groanings of the dying, and the curses of the living, who walked on in despair

... the army was in a wretched condition, from the want of provisions, shoes, and blankets; and insubordination began visibly to show its capricious front in more brigades than ours. When we got upon the mountainous roads we found them covered with deep snow; and our march that day was very long and fatiguing. When we halted, neither barracks nor convents offered us an asylum; the earth was our bed, the sky our covering, and the loud winds sang us to sleep.'

Next day, 31 December, the remaining regiments filed out of Astorga and into the mountains. William Surtees and the men of Craufurd's Brigade:

'... had been told to keep a sharp lookout on the Leon side of Astorga, for the enemy was every moment expected to make his appearance from that quarter; however, we were not disturbed during the short time we remained ... We continued our march from Astorga the same day and reached the village of Foncebadon, about twenty miles distant. Here we pigged in as well as we were able, there being only five or six houses; but as we had a few tents with us, we managed not amiss. Till now our brigade had formed the rear of the infantry, there being some cavalry in rear of us; but it was now determined that ours and the Light German Brigade under Brigadier-General Charles Alten, should strike off from the great road, and take the route for Orense and Vigo. This was done, I understand, with a view to secure a passage across the Miño at the former place, should Sir John, with the main army, be compelled to retreat in that direction, and probably with the view also of drawing off a part of the enemy's overwhelming force from the pursuit of that body, and to induce them to follow us into the mountains.'

Moore's decision to despatch the Light Brigades to the port of Vigo, south of Corunna, was a controversial one which has divided historians ever since. According to William Napier, Sir

John, lacking detailed information from his engineers, was still unsure which port – Corunna or Vigo – would make the best embarkation point for his army. In this context, the decision to detach a strong corps may be seen as a necessary evil, which Moore 'reluctantly adopted by the advice of his Quartermaster General'. Sir Charles Oman, however, believed the move to be a blunder, occasioned by a mistaken belief on the part of Moore, that the French would not pursue him beyond the mountains, due to exhaustion and lack of supplies. In this context, the expedition to Vigo may be seen, primarily, as an attempt to ease his own supply problems, worsening by the day on the Corunna road. In the event, however, the French pushed on, concentrating their might against Moore's reduced force as it limped towards Corunna, and leaving the Light Brigades to execute a long, lonely march to Vigo, harried only by hunger, fatigue and appalling weather. Thus, as Oman – with the benefit of hindsight – states, '3,500 fine soldiers were wasted for all fighting purposes.'

Meanwhile, back at Astorga, one of the last units to leave on the 31st was the 1st Battalion, 28th Regiment, whose men had spent the day destroying stores and equipment which, as ever, could not be removed for want of transport. According to Robert Blakeney, they left the town, 'with more headaches than full stomachs', and during the course of the evening, reached the small village of Cambarros, six miles out of Astorga. Here the weary soldiers hoped to bed down for the night, but as Blakeney later recalled, their stay:

> '...was but short, for scarcely had the men laid down to repose, which was much wanted in consequence of the manner in which they had passed the previous night, when some of our cavalry came galloping in, reporting that the enemy were advancing in force. We were immediately ordered to get under arms, and hurried to form outside the town on that part facing Bembibre. While we were forming a dragoon rode up, and an officer who being ill was in one of the light carts which attended the Reserve, cried out, "Dragoon, what news?" "News, sir? The only news I have for you

is that unless you step out like soldiers, and don't wait to pick your steps like bucks on Bond Street of a Sunday with shoes and silk stockings, damn it, you'll be all taken prisoners." "Pray, who the devil are you?" came from the cart. "I am Lord Paget," said the dragoon, "and pray, sir, may I ask who are you?" "I am Captain D__n, of the 28th Regiment, my lord." "Come out of that cart directly," said his Lordship. "March with your men, sir, and keep up their spirits by showing them a good example." The Captain scrambled out of the cart rear, face foremost, and from slipping along the side of the cart and off the wheels, and from the sudden jerks which he made to regain his equilibrium, displayed all the ridiculous motions of a galvanised frog.'

Lord Paget would shortly be *hors de combat* himself, following an attack of ophthalmia, which would temporarily render him almost blind.

Thus, in the dying hours of 1808, Astorga was clear of British troops. Twenty miles or so up the road, the men of the vanguard had hit the wine cellars of Bembibre, while the rest of the army toiled up the twisting mountain tracks in their wake. As for Romana, deprived of Moore's support, he had little choice but to quit town, electing to retire upon Orense, 100 miles to the west. And so Sir John had given Napoleon the slip once more – but only just. French troops were just fifteen miles behind and closing fast. On the morrow they would enter Astorga, still crammed with military stores, sick and wounded soldiers, plus several hundred stragglers, determined to get dead drunk.

Notes

1. Romana later claimed that there was no point in destroying the bridge at Mansilla, as the Esla was fordable in several places nearby.
2. General Martinengo was commander of the 2nd Division of Romana's Army of Galicia.

3. General Franceschi commanded this division of light cavalry, consisting of the 8th Dragoons, 22nd Chasseurs à Cheval, the Chasseurs Hannovrienne and the 1st Provisional Chasseurs à Cheval, some 2,200 sabres in all.

CHAPTER 6

Every Man for Himself and God for Us All!

Napoleon entered Astorga in the early hours of 1 January 1809, to find that his enemies (with the exception of several hundred invalids and inebriated stragglers) had vanished once again. Having linked up with Soult, the Emperor now fielded a force of some 70,000 men, supported by 200 guns. These colossal numbers – concentrated at such a cost in human misery – were of no avail, however, so long as his quarry remained out of reach. Napoleon resorted to propaganda, therefore, in an attempt to discredit Moore: caricatures, pamphlets, and songs, portraying the British as brutish, gutless drunkards, were to be circulated; false reports, claiming that the redcoats had sacked Leon (though they had not been within thirty miles of the place), were to be published; and the world was informed that Moore had abandoned the Spaniards, 'in a shameful and cowardly manner'.

Nothing could disguise the fact, however, that the Emperor's grand plan of encirclement and annihilation had come to naught. Moore had made the safety of the mountains and his eventual salvation – courtesy of the Royal Navy – seemed all but guaranteed. The 'English' must, of course, be pursued, harassed, and if possible, driven into the sea; but Napoleon, feeling such a task to be beneath his dignity, determined to go no further himself. Instead, he announced his immediate return to Paris, where, rather conveniently, affairs of state suddenly demanded his urgent personal intervention. From now on, Marshal Soult would be responsible for directing the campaign against Moore, which, from Napoleon's perspective, was beginning to whiff of failure.

In order to achieve his task of evicting the British from Spain, Soult would be left with the 20,000 men of II Corps, aided by a further 16,000 from Marshal Ney's VI Corps. The spearhead of this force would consist of the cavalry of Generals Colbert and Lahoussaye, supported by Merle's 1st Infantry Division. The remainder of the imperial host, however, was to be dispersed, some units marching back to Madrid, others heading south to crush the last pockets of patriotic resistance. Thus, the respite which Moore's diversion had bought for the Spaniards, was about to expire.

Meanwhile, in the mountains above Astorga, blizzards and sub-zero temperatures had replaced the recent rains, adding to the calamities of the retreating British, as William Green of the 1st Battalion, 95th Regiment, recalled:

> 'We had no tents . . . a blanket had been served out to each man; we marched from daylight until dark . . . our spirits so low with hunger and fatigue, that we often said we would as soon die as live.'

The cavalry and transport were equally badly off, as Charles Stewart observed:

> '. . . men and horses foundered at every step; the former worn out through fatigue and want of nutriment – the latter sinking under their loads, and dying upon the march. Nor was it the baggage-animals alone that suffered – the shoes of the cavalry horses dropped off, and consequently, they soon became useless. It was a sad spectacle to behold these fine creatures goaded on till their strength utterly failed them, and then shot to death by their riders, to prevent them from falling into the hands of the enemy. Then again, the few wagons which had hitherto kept up, fell, one by one, to the

rear; and the ammunition was destroyed and the carriages abandoned. Thus were misfortunes accumulated upon us as we proceeded; and it appeared improbable, should our present system of forced marches be continued, that one-half the army would ever reach the coast.'

In the midst of these miseries, some still cared about the passing of the old year and the birth of the new: 'This is New Year's Day,' mumbled an officer to his comrade, 'If we live to see another we shall not easily forget this one.' Others, like the Scottish 'Soldier of the 71st', could not help but contrast their own grim situation with that of fortunate friends, safe and sound at hearth and home:

> 'What a New Year's Day had we passed! Drenched with rain, famished with cold and hunger, ignorant when our misery was to cease. This was the most dreadful period of my life. How differently did we pass our Hogmanay from the manner our friends were passing theirs at home. Not a voice said, "I wish you a Happy New Year." Each seemed to look upon his neighbour as an abridgement to his own comforts. His looks seemed to say, "One or other of the articles you wear would be of great use to me; your shoes are better than those I possess; if you were dead, they would be mine..."'

This was a sentiment echoed by Benjamin Harris, who claimed that:

> 'There was no longer any endeavour to assist one another after a fall, it was every man for himself and God for us all!'

For many soldiers, mental anguish was added to the physical torment, with the knowledge that their women and children were trudging behind them, suffering even greater hardships than themselves. Army regulations permitted wives to follow their husbands to war in small numbers – five for every company of 100 men – and in return for their work as cooks, cleaners, and seamstresses, they were added to the company's ration-strength.

When Moore's expedition set off from Lisbon, however, many inexperienced regimental officers – from a misguided sense of sentimentality – had turned a blind eye to the flocks of females, determined to accompany their menfolk. As a consequence, the retreating columns were now pursued not only by the French, but also by a wretched army of women and children, blue with cold, ravaged by hunger, and with no official status. No longer able to ride on the supply wagons – which, as Stewart notes above, were being abandoned in large numbers for want of beasts to draw them – these poor creatures were obliged to pick up their possessions and march through the snow like soldiers. In many cases, the bitter weather was too much for frail bodies, worn down with want and weariness, to bear, as Harris recalled:

> 'I passed a man and woman lying in the snow, clasped in each other's arms. I knew them both because they belonged to the Rifles. It was Joseph Sitdown and his wife. Poor Sitdown had not been in good health prior to the retreat so he and his wife had been allowed to get on in front as best they could. But now they had given in and the last we ever saw of them was . . . lying perishing in each other's arms.'

In the late morning of 1 January, the vanguard quit Bembibre – leaving behind hundreds of stragglers who were literally too drunk to stand – and continued their trek to Villafranca, some twenty miles distant. Trudging through the snow in the blackest of humours, the officers criticised their absent commander-in-chief for abandoning Astorga without a fight; while the men, disconcerted by Moore's continued non-presence among their ranks, anxiously watched for signs of his appearance, repeatedly asking, 'Where's the general?' Sir John, however, was still on the road from Cambarros, marching with his friend, Sir Edward Paget, and the troops of the Reserve Division, which, on the departure of the Light Brigades, had effectively become the army's rearguard.

Although Moore attempted to boost the morale of these men with a mixture of stoicism and self-assurance, it was remarked that his features were grim and careworn, and that in moments of solitude, he wept for the plight of his men.

At the very rear of the column, trailing after Sir Edward Paget's Bembibre-bound infantry, rode Captain Gordon and the 15th Hussars. The remainder of the cavalry had been sent on ahead – horses being of little use in mountain country – leaving the 15th (reduced to between 300 and 400 mounted men) to fight off the French and hustle forward the stragglers unaided.

'If our Christmas was gloomy, the New Year did not afford us brighter prospects,' confided Gordon to his journal:

> 'On the contrary, our situation was become even more critical . . . Our difficulties and distresses increased at every league we marched, and the disorganisation of the troops became more apparent every day.'

Sadly, the British were becoming increasingly prone to vent their frustration at these 'difficulties' and 'distresses' on the long-suffering Spanish peasantry. When, for example, Gordon's troop reached the village of Mauregatos on the afternoon of 1 January, they found it a smouldering wreck:

> 'The wretched inhabitants were sitting amidst the trifling articles of property they had been able to save from the flames, contemplating the ruins of their houses in silent despair. The bodies of several Spaniards who had died of hunger or disease or perished from the inclemency of the weather, were lying scattered around, and heightened the horrors of the scene. The village had been burned by some of our infantry and scarcely an hour passed in which we did not witness the most pitiable misery, occasioned by the excesses of our troops, which it was impossible to prevent. Numbers continually straggled to the villages near the road, which, after pillaging, they generally set on fire; and whenever they discovered the places where wine was concealed, they drank until they

incapacitated themselves from rejoining the line of march or perished in the flames they had kindled. It is not surprising that this conduct excited in the breasts of the natives a detestation of the British, which induced them to retaliate, as often as they had the opportunity, by murdering or ill-treating the stragglers.'

Meanwhile, up the road at Bembibre, Deputy Assistant Commissary-General August Schaumann had arrived to find the 'wretched, filthy little hole' still packed with stupefied stragglers from the leading divisions. In fact, the place was so crammed with soused soldiery as to deny Schaumann a bed to rest his freezing, aching, limbs:

'At the cost of great pains I was able to stable my horse, or rather wedge it into one of the houses packed to the attics with men and beasts; while I myself crept into a dreadful house, where there was hardly enough room left to allow me to lie down and rest. I had brought with me a handkerchief full of rye, and on this I fed. I had also been able to procure a little bread on the road from a native, to whom I gave a dollar to fetch it from some hiding place he had. With this I now refreshed myself. Then laying myself resignedly on the bare floor among a number of exhausted stragglers, I wrapped myself in my cloak and was soon fast asleep, despite the fact that my boots and socks were wet through, and my teeth were chattering with the cold.'

Moore entered shortly after with the troops of the Reserve, one of whom, Robert Blakeney, mistakenly took the redcoats lying prostrate in the streets – crimson-coloured wine flowing from their lips and nostrils – for the casualties of some recent battle: 'Bembibre exhibited all the appearance of a place lately stormed and pillaged,' he later recalled. Meanwhile, Sir John sat on his horse silently fuming, his face like thunder, as Blakeney and his comrades set to work, 'turning or dragging the drunken men out of the houses into the streets, and sending forward as many as could be moved.' Yet it proved an almost impossible task, as 'little could be effected with men incapable of standing, much less of marching.'

Lieutenant-General Sir John Moore at the time of his appointment as commander of British forces in Spain. He was a consummate soldier and experienced in theatres as varied as the West Indies, Ireland and Egypt. *(Anne S. K. Brown Military Collection)*

Lord Henry William Paget. A hussar general
and man of considerable dash, Paget scored
success during the campaign at Sahagun and
Benavente.

General William Carr Beresford was another veteran and one of Moore's trusted subordinates. After the Corunna Campaign Beresford was sent to Portugal to train the Portuguese Army.

August Schaumann the young German commissary who left such a startling account of the retreat. Born in 1778 the Hanoverian served throughout the Peninsular War until retiring to Hanover in 1814. He was part of the commissary service, a much-neglected, and much-maligned, part of Britain's military machine.

Colonel Robert Craufurd, known as 'Black Bob', was a ferocious disciplinarian and a man much respected by the men under his command. Like Moore, Craufurd had learnt his trade in far-flung campaigns and, like Moore, he was to die in Spain – at Ciudad Rodrigo in 1812.

Marshal Soult, known to the British troops as the Duke of Damnation, led the French pursuit of Moore. The campaign was Soult's first experience of fighting a British force but he would encounter British troops throughout his Peninsular career.

General Charles Lefebvre-Desnouëttes, commander of Napoleon's Imperial Guard Chasseurs à Cheval, was at the forefront of the French pursuit until his capture at Benavente.

Moore's troops cross the Tagus on 1 November 1808 and enter Spain.
The crossing was unopposed and a relatively peaceful opening move to
the campaign.

Above: Lord Paget's hussars inflicted a sharp check on General Debelle's outposts at Sahagun, on 21 December 1808.

Above: Napoleon leads his men over the Guadarrama Mountains just sixty miles from Moore's position.

As the British advance turned into a retreat Moore's rearguard played
a decisive and demanding role. Here hussars deploy to cover the rear
as British columns fall back along muddy tracks.

An officer of the King's German Legion Hussars. The Legion, was composed of Hanoverian exiles, and formed an important part of British strength in the Peninsular War and, for Moore, the Legion's cavalry proved invaluable.

Chasseurs à Cheval of Napoleon's Imperial Guard struggle in the waters of the Esla at Benavente. It was here that General Lefebvre-Desnouëttes was captured.

The town of
Villafranca witnessed
the horror of the
British retreat in early
January 1809. Much
of the town was
consumed in fires
started by the drunken
soldiery.

British riflemen from Paget's 4th (Reserve) Division
skirmish in the snow during an episode of the retreat.

Above: Possibly the most famous image of the retreat, Beadle's study of Craufurd and the rearguard is a romanticised but powerful painting.

Above: This contemporary view of the battle of Corunna gives a good indication as to the confusion of the Napoleonic battlefield. The battle raged from 2.00 p.m. on 16 January until late that evening.
(Anne S. K. Brown Military Collection)

This image of the retreat shows the horrendous state of the roads and the terrain through which the troops – French and British alike – had to pass.

Highlanders and Frenchmen fight hand-to-hand in the streets of Elviña. The village was the scene of fierce fighting between the Royal Highland Foot and Mermet's Frenchmen.

Above: A view of Corunna harbour. The port was crowded with ships on the night of 14 January when over 100 naval transports gathered below the San Cristobal heights and Santa Margarita hills.
(Anne S. K. Brown Military Collection)

Above: A French sketch of the fighting at Corunna. In fact cavalry played a small part in the battle as the terrain was too difficult for the effective use of mounted troops.

Soult and his staff direct the assault on Corunna. British prisoners are being brought in on the left whilst the masts of the transports are just visible in the background.

Above: A French view of the battle which shows both sides pressing forward to attack. Indeed the nature of the fighting was of one attack being met and followed by a counter-attack.

Above: The voyage home took nearly two weeks for the exhausted, miserable survivors. Many of the soldiers were soon packed off on another bungled expedition – this time to Flushing in the Netherlands.

The burial of Sir John Moore by G. Jones. Moore's shoulder was shattered during the battle and he died that evening. Wrapped in his cloak he was buried near the citadel and his grave was later honoured by Soult and his generals.

On the morning of 2 January, Moore marched the Reserve out of Bembibre, leaving behind almost 1,000 befuddled men who, in spite of all efforts to move them, were simply too soused to stand. 'We had a great deal of trouble with the stragglers,' noted Captain Gordon, 'numbers of whom were so drunk that all our efforts to drive them on were fruitless and we were obliged to abandon them to their fate.' And a particularly cruel fate it was too. For almost as soon as their protectors had vanished from sight, the cavalry of the French advanced guard galloped into Bembibre and set about the slaughter of every human being in their way, as Napier remembered:

> '... in a moment the road was filled with the miserable stragglers who came crowding after the troops, some with shrieks of distress and wild gestures, others with brutal exclamations, while many, overcome with fear, threw away their arms, while those who preserved them were too stupidly intoxicated to fire, and kept reeling to and fro, alike insensible to their danger and to their disgrace.'

The doom of these hapless revellers, however, was sealed, as Gordon later lamented:

> 'They were soon overtaken by the French *chasseurs* who treated them most unmercifully, cutting to their right and left, and sparing none who came within reach of their swords. They were even accused of wounding the sick men whom they overtook in the hospital wagons.'

A few maimed and lacerated survivors made the safety of the British column, their injuries arousing howls of horror, pity, and outrage. Moore made public exhibits of them, in the hope that their shocking wounds might deter others from quitting the colours. Charles Stewart was barely able to hide his disgust:

> 'I am sure that British troops never looked upon a spectacle more appalling than those few presented who, having come up with the column, bleeding and

mangled by sabre cuts, were, by order of the General, paraded through the ranks as a warning to their comrades.'

Meanwhile, the men of the vanguard poured into Villafranca, desperate for food, drink, and shelter. The town was one of Moore's main depots, containing two weeks' worth of rations, numerous stores, and hundreds of barrels of rum. But, with insufficient transport to remove these much-needed supplies, and little time to effect their distribution, Moore had ordered their destruction by fire, that they might not fall into the hands of the French. This drastic step, however, provoked an avalanche of despair among the troops – many of whom were as wretched as beggars – and their exasperation boiled over into bedlam. August Schaumann, who arrived in the early evening of 2 January, described the scene as the town teetered on the brink of anarchy:

'Although Villafranca is not small, every corner of it was soon full of men. You could hardly turn round in the place, and many regiments had to bivouac. Most of the mules and draft-bullocks and pack-horses seemed only to have lasted out up to this point, and now fell down and died. Very soon we could neither drive nor ride through many of the streets. The rations came to an end, but, amid the chaos that reigned, could in any case no longer have been distributed. Fresh troops were always streaming in, the stores depots were also violently raided, and the commissaries were no longer able to perform their duties. In the end Villafranca was literally plundered, and the drunkenness that prevailed among the troops led to the most shameful incidents. Down by the river the artillery destroyed their stores, and lighting big fires burnt all their ammunition wagons, which they broke up for the purpose. They also threw all their ammunition into the river. Several hundred horses, which could go no further, were led to the same spot and shot. Day and night we could hear the sound of

114

pistol fire. Everything was destroyed. Discipline was at an end, and the officers were no longer heeded.'

All were now absorbed with their own personal miseries, their own personal hells. For the 'Private of the 42nd', contemplating his bare and bloodstained feet, life had been reduced to a desperate hunt for a pair of boots:

'I was in great hopes of getting a pair of shoes, but there was no time for shoes and spirits to be given us, though there was plenty of both in the store. There were a great many of the men who got shoes, but it was by forcing their way into the store, and breaking the casks in which the shoes were packed up. When I saw this, I endeavoured to get a pair; but the crowd was so great, I could not get near the entrance, and I could not tarry, for the bugle was sounding to fall in. The provost then came with his guard of horse, and cleared the store. In a short time, notwithstanding our wretchedness and wants, and bleeding feet, all that was in the store was destroyed. I would to God that I had seen no other than this of "man's inhumanity to man." There was a man of the company I belonged to that got three pairs of shoes; I offered him three dollars, all the money I had, for a pair: the rascal would not give them to me, expecting more for them before we got to Corunna.'

Villafranca was soon filled to capacity, yet the redcoats continued to pour in. Unable to find billets at the crowded convents and churches, some destitute soldiers began a spree of house-breaking, in order to solve the accommodation crisis – sometimes with alarming consequences.

'When we came to Villafranca, the Spaniards shut their houses on us,' recalled Sergeant Miller of the Royal Regiment of Artillery:

'Me and four more broke open a house where they had plenty of wood but they would not give us any. I went downstairs to take some but they had some Spanish soldiers to guard it. They said, one to the other, "kill

him" and began to push me about. I asked them in
Spanish if that was the treatment they meant to give us
after fighting for them. One of them very luckily
pushed me against the stairs. I immediately ran up and
told the four men to be on their guard or we should
be all killed. One placed himself behind the door and
I and the other three stood with our swords drawn. In
a few minutes after, up came three Spanish soldiers
with large staves and knives. The man behind the door
ran one of them through and I cut down another and
the third had three swords on him. We left them all for
dead. Soon after, we heard a great noise in pulling
them away and next morning at daylight when we
marched away we saw a deal of blood on the stairs,
which made us think they were all killed, which they
very justly deserved.'

Moore appeared in the evening, to find the town – in the
words of Stewart – 'filled with drunken and disorderly men,
by whom the most violent outrages had been committed, not
only upon the natives but upon our own magazines.'
Despairing at the shocking scenes which met his eyes, Moore
resolved to bring the troops sharply to heel. As it happened,
two or three troopers of the 18th Hussars were caught in the
act of looting under Sir John's very nose and, for the sake of
example, he ordered that one of them be shot. But as Stewart
points out:

'. . . the discipline of the army was by this time too
much impaired to be seriously affected by example,
similar offences were committed whenever
opportunities occurred; and with the recklessness of
men who fancied that their case was desperate.'

For Moore, however, the case was even more desperate, as
he watched his army fall apart before his eyes. Hearing of
outbreaks of lawlessness among the previously steady troops of
the Reserve, Sir John immediately rushed to the scene, in
order to nip any further trouble in the bud. Sir Edward
Paget's men had been halted six miles out of town, at the
village of Cacabellos, at a spot where the highroad crossed the

River Cua. Robert Blakeney remembered the Reserve being halted in a field by the side of the road, when Moore:

> '...rode up and addressed us in the most forcible and pathetic manner. After dwelling on the outrageous disorders and want of discipline in the army, he concluded by saying, "And if the enemy are in possession of Bembibre, which I believe, they have got a rare prize. They have taken or cut to pieces many hundred drunken British cowards – for none but unprincipled cowards would get drunk in presence, nay, in the very sight of the enemies of their country; and sooner than survive the disgrace of such infamous misconduct, I hope that the first cannon-ball fired by the enemy may take me in the head." Then turning to us, he added: "And you, 28th, are not what you used to be. You are not the regiment who to a man fought by my side in Egypt. If you were, no earthly temptation could even for an instant seduce one of you away from your colours." He then rode off and returned to Villafranca. This feeling and pungent address made a deep impression on every individual present ... but the feeling of remorse was but of short duration – future temptations brought on future disorders.'

As darkness fell, Captain Gordon and the 15th Hussars – bringing up the rear as usual – entered the abandoned village of Cubilos on the Villafranca road. Here, a company of the 1st Battalion, 95th Rifles, was engaged in a hot skirmish with a French cavalry patrol, and the hussars were obliged to pitch in and put the intruders to flight. Thereafter, the regiment quit the village and bivouacked on the highroad, their pickets so close to those of the French, that pistol and carbine shots were exchanged sporadically throughout the night. The weather was intensely cold, but the troopers had found food and fuel in Cubilos, and soon settled down by several blazing fires.

In the dead of night, however, the sentries were alarmed by the shadow of a creature, creeping through the undergrowth by the side of the road. At first, they took their uninvited guest for a wild pig, but closer inspection revealed – to their horror

– a survivor of the morning's massacre at Bembibre. Without further ado, the poor creature was led to the light of the officers' fire, where, according to Captain Gordon:

'[He] ...presented the most shocking spectacle I ever beheld. It was impossible to distinguish a single feature. The flesh of his cheeks and lips was hanging in collops; his nose was slit and his ears, I think, were cut off. Besides the wounds on his head, he had received many in different parts of the body and it is surprising that he should have been able to make his escape in the feeble state to which he was reduced by loss of blood ...The unfortunate man was unable to swallow solid food but we gave him some warm wine and when he was a little revived by the heat of the fire, he was sent to the hospital at Villafranca; but I imagine he had little chance of recovering. In addition to his wounds, it is probable that his limbs were frostbitten; for it was quite horrible to see the manner in which he cowered near the fire and raked the glowing embers towards him with his fingers. It was with difficulty he could make himself understood but we learnt from him that the loiterers had been most barbarously treated by the enemy.'

CHAPTER 7

Bayonets Crossed and Blood Profusely Drawn

On the morning of 3 January, the market square at Villafranca was crowded with British troops, called to witness the execution of one of the cavalry troopers caught looting the previous day. Among the crush of silent spectators stood Commissary clerk, August Schaumann:

> 'I was told that General Moore ...was so much exasperated by the relaxed discipline and the excesses that had taken place, that he was going to make an example of the fellow. It appeared that in a certain house three hussars had broken open a case, and extracted a ham and other things from it. Thousands of others had done the same, and much worse. Unfortunately, however, General Moore happened to be riding through the street when the Spaniards raised their outcry over the ham, and these three fellows had had to draw lots for their lives. The man who lost was led out, and placed in a kneeling position with his face turned towards a big tree. A detachment of twenty men stood behind him with their carbines at the ready. In a loud voice the adjutant cried, "Fire!" and the poor devil was dead; whereupon all the troops were made to march past the corpse.'

Having delivered a brutal, bloody warning to his troops, Sir John ordered them out of town and back onto the Corunna road, but according to the 'Soldier of the 71st':

> 'Great numbers would not leave the town, but concealed themselves in the wine cellars, which they had broken open, and were left there.'

Others, however – including a certain Commissariat man by the name of Moore – were only too pleased to decamp. An irascible bully, Commissary Moore could only be cowed by his even more formidable spouse, and a crowd of bemused onlookers attended their bungled flight, as Schaumann observed:

> 'He had his gig brought out, and tried to get his luggage onto it but owing to the tumult he could not succeed, and being a notoriously choleric person, he went almost mad with rage. His wife, a fat woman, who was looking out of the window implored him to be more patient, and urged him above all to be calm and keep his presence of mind. But she was nicely rewarded for her pains; for never in my life shall I again hear a flow of choice invective as this fellow Moore poured forth against her. Now, however, it was her turn to lose patience, and she retaliated with such a volley of exquisite abuse – she was an Irishwoman – which, by the bye, she punctuated by flinging down all sorts of missiles, consisting of cups and pots and pans, upon his head, that all those who were standing by, even the wounded, were contorted with laughter.'

In the midst of this mayhem, preparations were made to spoil any stores, provisions, or equipment which could not be carried away. Sergeant Benjamin Miller, of the Royal Artillery, noted in his journal that as many as 500 wagon-loads of ammunition and kit – including the men's knapsacks – were earmarked for destruction:

> 'So now we were light enough, our backs almost bare, our bellies empty and no shoes to our feet. Our

greatest burden was the Spanish lice; the few rags we
had left were covered with them.'

Meanwhile, as the bulk of the army made ready to retire,
the Reserve Division was still posted six miles down the road
at Cacabellos, a settlement of some 150 houses straddling the
Bembibre road. Their position was a strong one. A series of
low hills commanded the approaches to the village, ruling out
the possibility of a surprise attack from the east; through its
centre ran the River Cua, the banks of which were lined with
vineyards, enclosed by a network of walls and hedges, offering
ideal cover for sharpshooters; the banks of the river were
connected by a narrow stone bridge, over which ran the main
Bembibre–Villafranca highway; and the bridge itself was
commanded by more high ground on the western or
Villafranca shore, making it a potentially deadly defile for an
enemy to negotiate. Sir John's engineers had already suggested
the spot as a prime site for battle, but Moore no longer
believed his men capable of fighting a major action. Instead,
the five infantry regiments of Paget's Reserve, augmented by
the 15th Hussars and a battery of artillery, were tasked with
keeping the French at bay, while the vanguard extricated itself
from Villafranca.

Paget's advanced pickets consisted of soldiers from the 1st
Battalion, 95th, and the 15th Hussars – some 700 men in all –
posted several miles in advance of his position. They had spent
the morning skirmishing with General Colbert's cavalry
brigade, also around 700 strong and consisting of the 15th
Chasseurs à Cheval and the 3rd Hussars. At noon, a wounded
chasseur was brought before Colonel Colquhoun Grant,[1] of the
15th Hussars. After pleading with his captors for kind
treatment, the Frenchman divulged the alarming news that the
British outposts would soon be facing Soult's entire advanced
guard, as Colbert was hourly expecting the arrival of 1,000
dragoons under General Lahoussaye, and 4,500 infantrymen
under General Merle.

Captain Gordon recalled that this information was soon
seemingly confirmed:

'I was conversing with Colonel Grant at the time, and
in a few minutes Captain Thackwell joined us with the
intelligence that the French were in motion and that
twenty squadrons could be distinctly counted in their
lines.'

Appreciating the urgency of the situation, Colonel Grant
invited Sir John Slade (in overall command of the cavalry that
day, since Lord Paget and General Stewart were both now
suffering from ophthalmia) to ride forward with him and take
a closer look. The General declined, however, insisting that he
should fly to Villafranca forthwith, and personally acquaint
Moore with the latest developments. Somewhat bemused by
this response, Gordon and his fellow officers looked on as
Slade:

'... clapped spurs to his horse and was quickly out of
sight. We learned that he did not slacken his pace until
he met Sir John Moore, to whom he repeated what he
had heard, saying that he was desired by Colonel
Grant to report it. Sir John Moore asked the Brigadier
how long he had been Colonel Grant's *aide-de-camp* and
told him that the proper post of a general officer was
at the head of his brigade or division when in presence
of the enemy. The General, however, considered the
Tenth as the head of his brigade, for we saw no more
of him.'

Over the course of the next hour, General Colbert – who
had, in fact, elected to move against the British without
waiting for his supports to come up – cautiously advanced up
the Bembibre road towards Cacabellos. Gordon explained
how the 15th Hussars, who assumed they had a much larger
force to reckon with than was actually the case, steadily
withdrew in their turn:

'We retired very slowly, to allow the Reserve time to
break up their encampment, and the enemy followed
at the same pace along the highroad, with a band of
music playing at the head of their column. . . '

Back at Cacabellos, however, General Sir Edward Paget was more concerned with matters of discipline, than the imminent arrival of the 6,000 soldiers of Soult's advanced guard. At thirty-three years of age, Sir Edward – Lord Henry's younger brother and fourth son of the Earl of Uxbridge – was one of Moore's most charismatic lieutenants. Addicted to snuff and plagued by gout and rheumatism, Paget was, nevertheless, a force to be reckoned with, being possessed of supreme confidence and a fearsome temper. He had forbidden his men to enter Cacabellos (as a punishment for increasing disorder within their ranks) and yet it had come to his attention that several malefactors had been seized in the night while attempting to break into the villagers' houses and cellars. Now Paget – who considered flogging a universal panacea – intended to make them suffer. Robert Blakeney was an eyewitness:

> 'Early on the morning of the 3rd the Reserve marched up towards the crown of a low hill, in front of Cacabellos on the Bembibre side. Here we halted, leaving so much of it above us as served to screen us from the view of an approaching foe. No enemy having as yet advanced, the General ordered a hollow square to be formed, facing inwards. A drumhead court martial sat in rear of every regiment, and within the square were placed the triangles.[2] The culprits seized in the town, as soon as tried and sentenced, were tied up, and a general punishment took place along the four faces of the square; and this continued for several hours. During this time our *vedettes* came in frequently to report to the General that the enemy were advancing. His only reply was, "Very well." The punishment went on.'

Eventually, two men found guilty of robbing a Spaniard were brought forward, and having been sentenced to death by Paget, were led with ropes round their necks to a tall tree, situated in a corner of the square. Here they were hoisted onto the shoulders of the Provost-Marshal's men, while the ropes were attached to the branches. At this point, however, the proceedings were interrupted by the sudden appearance of 'a cavalry officer of high regimental rank',[3] who galloped into the centre of the square. This unexpected saviour was none other than a puce and panting Sir John Slade, come to inform Paget of the advancing French menace. According to Blakeney:

> 'General Paget was then silent for a few moments, and apparently suffering under great excitement. He at length addressed the square by saying: "My God! Is it not lamentable to think that, instead of preparing the troops confided to my command to receive the enemies of their country, I am preparing to hang two robbers? But though that angle of the square should be attacked, I shall execute these villains in this angle!" The General again became silent for a moment, and our pickets were heard retiring up the opposite side of the hill and along the road which flanked it on our left. After a moment's pause he addressed the men a second time in these words: "If I spare the lives of these two men, will you promise to reform?" Not the slightest sound, not even breathing, was heard within the square. The question was repeated: "If I spare the lives of these men, will you give me your word of honour as soldiers that you will reform?" The same awful silence continued until some of the officers whispered to the men to say "Yes," when that word loudly and rapidly flew through the square. The culprits were then hastily taken away.'

And so, at about 1.00 p.m., with Colbert closing in on Cacabellos, Paget hustled his troops down the snow-clad hill and across the Cua to the safety of the western bank. Here, screened by the vineyard walls, his infantry fanned out into extended order, while the six guns of Carthew's artillery battery were wheeled into position astride the road commanding the bridge. Moments later, Colbert's troopers poured over the brow of the recently-vacated hill, pursuing the riflemen and hussars of Paget's pickets into Cacabellos itself. It was at this point that, according to Captain Gordon, the 15th

Hussars made a stand, fighting their foes hand-to-hand for every inch of ground:

> 'For some minutes we were so jammed together in a narrow street that it was impossible for either party to advance or retire. At this period of the conflict one of our men decapitated a French *chasseur* at a single blow; the head was not entirely separated, but remained attached by a muscle or part of the skin of the neck.'

Nevertheless, the flood of French horsemen proved too much for Gordon and his comrades and they eventually broke, stampeding through the ranks of retreating riflemen (as well as a number of panic-stricken staff officers out on reconnaissance) and making a mad dash for the bridge. There they became entangled with the Light Company of the 28th, which had been left on the hostile bank in order to cover the bridge until the last elements of the Reserve were safely across. Blakeney described the scene with typical British understatement:

> 'The situation of the Light Company was now very embarrassing, in danger of being trampled by our own cavalry, who rode over everything which came in their way, and crowded by the 95th and liable to be shot by them, for in their confusion they were firing in every direction. Some of them were a little the worse for liquor . . . and we were so mixed up with them and our own cavalry that we could offer no formation to receive the enemy, who threatened to cut us down. At length, the crowd dissipating, we were plainly to be seen by the French, who, probably taking us for the head of an infantry column, retired.'

This timely respite permitted the medley of badly shaken British troops to scramble across the bridge and form up on the opposite bank.

As for Colbert's men, though they had hacked down several British hussars and taken forty-eight riflemen prisoner, they had become hopelessly disorganised during the mêlée at the bridge, and had been recalled by their commander in order to rally, prior to the launching of another sortie.

At the age of thirty-one, General Auguste-François-Marie de Colbert was one of Napoleon's youngest generals and reputedly the most handsome man in Europe. He had formed a poor opinion of British soldiers – having seen no other specimen but drunken stragglers – and even though he knew the far bank to be defended, dismissed the danger as minimal. Addicted to glory, and burning with a desire to distinguish himself, Colbert arrayed his column four abreast, and prepared to carry the bridge by a frenzied onslaught.

Blakeney and the rest of his company were now nestling beneath the guns of Carthew's battery, and he described what then followed:

> 'Shortly after we had gained our position the French cavalry advanced at a quick trot down the hill. Our guns instantly wheeled out upon the road, and played upon their column until they became screened from their fire by the dip in the road as they approached the bridge. Here they were warmly received by the 52nd Regiment, now freed from our own dragoons, and the 95th; and upon this they made a furious charge at full speed over the bridge and up the road towards our position. During this onset they were severely galled by the 95th, who by this time had lined the hedges on either side of the road within a few yards of their flanks, and by the Light Company immediately in their front, whom it was evidently their intention to break through, as they rode close to our bayonets. But their ranks being much thinned by the destructive flanking fire of the rifles and of the standing ranks of the Light Company, their charge was vain, and they wheeled about and underwent the same ordeal in retiring, so that but few survived to tell the tragic tale. The road was absolutely choked with their dead. One alone among the slain was regretted, their gallant leader, General Colbert; his martial appearance, noble figure, manly gesture, and above all his daring bravery called forth the admiration of all.'

Blakeney's account suggests that General Colbert met his death during the mad charge across the bridge, into the mouths of the British guns. Indeed, both Napier and Oman – the two great Peninsular War historians – follow this line. However, an alternative version of Colbert's demise may be found in David Johnson's book, *The French Cavalry, 1792–1815.* According to Johnson, Colbert was still alive at 4.00 p.m., when, having extricated his brigade from the abortive attack on the bridge, he rode forward to encourage a party of skirmishers near the water's edge. Mindful that the general was 'offering much too good a target', one of Colbert's officers warned him not to take unnecessary risks: '"What's the matter?" Colbert chaffed him. "You seem unusually afraid of dying today!"' Seconds later, a bullet entered his skull above the left eyebrow.

If some controversy exists as to the time and location of Colbert's death, there is absolutely no doubt as to who brought him down. All the sources agree that the dashing French hothead was shot:

> '. . . by a noted pickle of the name of Tom Plunket, who, fearless of all danger to himself, got sufficiently nigh to make sure of his mark, and shot him, which, with the fire of the others, caused great havoc in the enemy's ranks, and set them flying to the rear much faster than they advanced.'[4]

According to a fellow marksman of the 95th, Plunket, an Irishman, was:

> '. . . a smart, well-made fellow, about middle height and in the prime of manhood; with a clear grey eye and handsome countenance. He was a general favourite with both officers and men, besides being the best shot in the regiment.'[5]

A story soon began to circulate that Plunket had been offered cash to kill Colbert by a high-ranking officer and Sir Edward Paget was named. Needless to say, the rumour was strenuously denied by the British top brass. Nevertheless,

Chapter 7

Edward Costello – a soldier of the 95th who was not present at Cacabellos – saw fit to repeat the tale in his memoirs, *Adventures of a Soldier*:

> 'A French general named Colbert, conspicuous on a grey horse, was remarkably active. Although frequently aimed at by our men, he seemed to bear a charmed life, and invariably escaped. In one of the French charges headed by this daring officer, General Paget rode up to the Rifles and offered his purse to any man who would shoot him. Plunket immediately started from his company. He ran about 100 yards nearer to the enemy, threw himself on his back on the road (which was covered with snow), placed his foot in the sling of his rifle, and taking deliberate aim, shot General Colbert. Colbert's trumpet-major,[6] who rode up to him, shared the same fate from Tom's unerring rifle ... Our general immediately gave Tom the purse he had promised, with encomiums upon his gallantry.'

Shortly after the spectacular failure of the French light cavalry to take the bridge of Cacabellos by storm, Moore arrived on the scene, having, Blakeney tells us, 'left Villafranca as soon as he heard the report of the first gun fired.' Sir John's entrance coincided with the appearance of Generals Lahoussaye and Merle on the opposite slope where, earlier that day, Paget had presided over his drumhead court martial. Consequently, it was not long, according to Oman, before the British were tested by a second assault, spearheaded by Lahoussaye's dragoons:

> '... several squadrons of them forded the river at different points, but unable to charge among the rocks and vines, they were forced to dismount and to act as skirmishers, a capacity in which they competed to no great advantage against the 52nd, with whom they found themselves engaged.'

With dusk descending, Merle sought to retrieve the situation by sending his light troops in support of the hard-pressed dragoons, as Blakeney remembered:

'The fight now became confused and the enemy's numbers increased every instant. Cavalry, *tirailleurs*, *voltigeurs*, 95th, and those of the 52nd Regiment who flew to the aid of their friends, now formed one indiscriminate mass.'

This chaotic scrap along the banks of the Cua continued for over an hour, when, at last, Merle dispatched a dense column of infantrymen towards the bridge. Charles Stewart describes how they were repulsed:

'The artillery attached to the Reserve instantly opened fire upon it and such was the excellence of the practice, that the enemy's column, after a heavy loss, withdrew before it had been able to fire a musket.'

Darkness finally put an end to the fighting at Cacabellos – which had claimed around 200 casualties on either side – and under its cover, Moore evacuated the position, as Charles Stewart commented:

'Sir John Moore was not desirous of bringing on a general action. He had heard of a position near Lugo, of which he proposed to take advantage. He neither wished to waste time, nor sacrifice lives, in the obstinate maintenance of ground to which he attached no value and therefore the Reserve was ordered to Villafranca – the main body to Herrerias – and it was followed, at ten o'clock, by the rearguard, which reached its halting-place soon after midnight.'

But a change had come over the British troops. Invigorated by battle and the feeling that they had avenged comrades butchered at Bembibre, they quit the field of Cacabellos immune, for a while at least, to the effects of hunger, cold, and exhaustion. The final words of this chapter belong to Robert Blakeney, who, though writing in his retirement, was, on 3 January 1809, barely twenty years of age:

'Thus it was that, when on this day the French infantry first came in close contact with ours, when bayonets were crossed and blood profusely drawn, our men were so wild and hot for the fray that it was hard to drag them from the field ... That Britons will fight to the last – that is, while they can stand – is well known; and it was this determination that caused Napoleon at the Battle of Waterloo to say that the English were beaten according to every rule of war, but did not know it.'

Notes

1. Lieutenant-Colonel Sir Colquhoun Grant (1764–1835) was appointed to the command of the 15th Hussars in August 1808. He should not be confused with the Lieutenant-Colonel Colquhoun Grant (1780–1829) who later served in Spain as Wellington's intelligence chief.
2. A reference to the pikes or halberds carried by sergeants and lashed together to form a kind of tripod. These makeshift frames were used to support the bodies of men sentenced to flogging. The number of lashes inflicted upon offenders could vary considerably: 300 was common and 700 not unknown. On occasion, 1,200 lashes were administered as a form of capital punishment.
3. Blakeney, Robert, *A Boy in the Peninsular War.*
4. Surtees, William, *Twenty-five Years in the Rifle Brigade.*
5. Costello, Edward, *Adventures of a Soldier.*
6. According to Sir Charles Oman, among others, this man was actually Colbert's *aide-de-camp*, Latour-Maubourg.

CHAPTER 8

The March of Death

During the night of 3 January, Moore's force concentrated at Herrerias, just beyond Villafranca. The dregs of the army remained behind, however, being either incapacitated by drink or bent on acquiring booty. Captain Gordon witnessed the scene as he passed through Villafranca with his troop of hussars:

> 'Parties of drunken soldiers were committing all kinds of enormities. Several houses were in flames and a quantity of baggage and military stores, for which there was no means of conveyance, were burning in the plaza. The kennels [*sic*] were flowing with rum, a number of puncheons having been staved in the streets and a promiscuous rabble were drinking and filling bottles and canteens from the stream.'

The flames spread quickly in the ensuing chaos and when Robert Blakeney arrived from the field of Cacabellos in the dead of night, he noted that, 'The whole town seemed on fire.' Nevertheless, Blakeney and his comrades of the Reserve marched across Villafranca *en route* for Herrerias; and though they had not touched a morsel of food all day, were paraded past piles of provisions which, doomed for want of transport, were in the process of being set alight:

'...and so tenacious were the Commissariat in preserving everything for the flames that they had guards posted around even the biscuits and salt meat to prevent the men as they passed from taking anything away ...But notwithstanding these precautions and strict orders and the chastisement received in the morning, many of the men had the hardihood as they passed, to stick their bayonets, and sergeants their pikes, into the salt pork, which was actually being set fire to. Several junks [portions of salt meat] were thus taken away, and many of the officers who cut and slashed at the men to prevent such sacrilege against the Commissariat *auto da fe*,[1] were very thankful that night at Herrerias, to get a small portion of the salt meat thus carried off.'

According to most sources, it was on the following day, 4 January, that Sir John finally chose between Vigo and Corunna as his army's point of departure. As previously noted, Moore had been keeping both options open, while awaiting the verdict of Fletcher, his Chief Engineer. Sir John was aware that the Royal Navy favoured Vigo, and had made a half-hearted concession by ordering his leading divisions to strike south for this port on reaching Lugo, some sixty miles north-west of Villafranca. But with Soult still on his tail, Moore was becoming less concerned with pleasing the Admiralty than selecting a port which could be adequately defended. It was with some relief, then, that Fletcher made his appearance at Herrerias with the welcome news that Corunna fitted the bill. Not only was it closer than Vigo, it offered a far stronger position from which to cover an embarkation. Moore concurred without a qualm and the matter was settled:

'The march to Vigo was therefore abandoned, the ships directed round to Corunna, and the General, who now deeply regretted the separation of his Light Brigades, sent forward instructions for the leading divisions to halt at Lugo, where he designed to rally the army and give battle if the enemy would accept it.'[2]

These instructions – addressed to the generals of the vanguard in advance of Herrerias – were placed in the hands of Captain George Napier, Sir John's *aide-de-camp*.[3] Napier bumped into Sir David Baird's 1st Division some twenty miles up the road at Nogales. Baird – an infamously bad tempered Scot – was in bed and received the captain with some ill-humour. The contents of Moore's missive did nothing to improve the general's mood, as he had consistently championed Vigo over Corunna as the army's point of exit; and when Napier offered to ride after General Fraser (whose 3rd Division, having passed through Lugo, was already a day's march down the road to Vigo), a grumpy Sir David declined, preferring to entrust the crucial despatch to a private dragoon. This man, as it turned out, got blind drunk on the road and the vital packet was lost. This fiasco remained undiscovered till the following morning and, though fresh orders were immediately dashed off, the damage – as Oman observes – was already done:

> 'Baird's negligence cost Fraser's battalions 400 men in stragglers, and having marched and counter-marched more than twenty miles, they returned to Lugo so thoroughly worn out that they could not possibly have resumed their retreat on the 6th.'

Charles Stewart, meanwhile, goes so far as to claim that a number of horses attached to Fraser's Division actually dropped dead upon re-entering the streets of Lugo, 'and even of the men, more than one were known to have perished of absolute exhaustion.'

Meanwhile, in the early evening of 4 January, Moore's rearguard – in the shape of Sir Edward Paget's Reserve Division – was only just approaching Nogales, having set off from Herrerias at break of day. Progress had been hindered by hordes of stragglers from the leading divisions, all of whom had to be rounded up and sent forward, and by the need to await the pickets of the 95th, who were hurrying up from Cacabellos, under constant pressure from the advancing French. As dusk fell, one of Paget's units – the Light Company of the 28th Regiment – came across a convoy of abandoned carts, stuck in the snow by the side of the road. Upon closer inspection the carts were found to contain heaps of uniforms, shoes, and weapons for the phantom Spanish armies. The scarecrow-soldiers of the 28th could hardly believe their luck, and immediately fell upon the stranded kit, only to be dragged off again by punctilious officers and herded back onto the road.

Senselessly denied the shoes and clothing they so desperately needed, the men limped into Nogales long after dark, cold, hungry and exhausted. But there was no warm welcome awaiting them. On the contrary, the inhabitants (having doubtless suffered at the hands of the vanguard) remained shut up inside their homes with doors and windows double-bolted. Ensign Robert Blakeney and the men of the light company were determined, however, not to be denied a billet:

> 'To force a Spanish door is not easy. They have large nails driven through the panels at small intervals; these nails, or rivets, have heads on the outer side of the doors nearly the size of a half-crown piece. And the doors are very massive, made of hardwood, generally oak, so that striking against them with the butt ends of the muskets was totally useless. On this occasion, after knocking for some time to no purpose, we took a large stone and, putting it into a sergeant's sash, four men stood close to the door supporting the sash, which formed a kind of sling; others pulled away the stone as far as the length of the sash permitted, and then, adding all their force to its return, sent it with a tremendous bump bang against the door. After we (for I acted engineer on the occasion) had repeated this mode of rapping five or six times, the door became uneasy on its hinges, and the master of the house put his head out of a window, as if just awakened, and began to remonstrate loudly against the outrage; upon which some of the men, in their desperation, threatened to shoot him at the window; and I believe that – had his remonstrances continued much longer –

I should have found it difficult to prevent their carrying the threat into execution. However, it could not have been held malice prepense,[4] since the muskets were always loaded; and as to manslaughter or justifiable homicide, they were practising it every hour. The door being at length wheeled back on its tottering hinges, we hurried into the house; and so uncouth we were under the circumstances – fatigued, fasting, and freezing – that before we enquired after the master's health, the welfare of his wife and family, or whether he had any such, he was closely interrogated as to the state of his larder and cellar. It is lucky that we were even so far courteous, as it was the last house we entered during the retreat.'

Having found food, warmth and shelter, the weary soldiers settled down to rest. The cramped conditions of the house, however, meant that Blakeney and his brother officers were quartered close by the men and obliged to endure their banter. A certain private soldier, known to his comrades as 'Gentleman' Roach, on account of his pompous airs and graces, chose this particular moment to hold forth on the beloved subject of his venerable ancestors. Roach was not a popular man with his down-to-earth Irish comrades, however, who had little faith in his martial qualities, and even less in his fanciful tales, as Blakeney recalled:

'Being no longer able to bear with his noise and vanity one of the men interrupted him by crying out: "Bad luck to you and all your ancisthors put together! I wish you'd hould your jaw, and let us lie quiet a little before the day comes, for we can hardly hould up our heads with the sleep." The "Gentleman", always put on his mettle at the mention of his ancestors, with indignant voice exclaimed: "Wretch! you personify all the disproportions of a vulgar cabbage-plant, the dense foliage of whose plebeian head is too ponderous for its ignoble crouching stem to support." "Faith, then," replied the plebeian, "I wish we had a good hid o' cabbage to ate now, and we'd give you the shrinking part, that's like yourself, good-for-nothing and not able

135

to stand when wanted; and, damn your sowl, what are you like, always talking about your rotten ould ancisthors? Sure, if you were any good yourself, you wouldn't be always calling them to take your part. Be Jabers! you're like a praty, for all your worth in the world is what's down in the ground!" "Contemptible creature!" replied the "Gentleman", "if even the least of my noble line of ancestors were to rise from the grave, he would display such mighty feats of arms as would astound you and all the vulgar herd of which you appear to be the appropriate leader." The conclusion of this contemptuous speech being accompanied with a revolving glance, and his right arm put into a semi-circular motion, including all the men as it passed through its orbit, brought him many adversaries. One of his new antagonists bellowed out with a loud laugh: "Bury him, bury him! Since all the bravery that belongs to him is with his ould dads in the ground; maybe, if we buried him a little while to make an ould ancisthor of him too, and then dug him up again, he might be a good soldier himself!" "Arrah! sure it's no use," cried out another, "to be loosing your talk with a dancing-master like him. Wasn't he squeezed up behind a tree, like the back of an old Cramona fiddle, while I was bothering three Johnny Craps, when they were running down screaming like pelebeens to charge the bridge? And, after all that, I'll engage with his rotten ould ancisthors that when he goes home he'll have a bether pinshun than me, or be made a sergeant by some fine curnil that always stays at home and knows nothing at all about a good soldier. . . ""

A short time later – much to Blakeney's relief – the debate died down and most of the men were overtaken by sleep. There were some, however, who chose to forego the luxury of unconsciousness. Stealing silently away from the settlement and into the blackness beyond, they retraced their former route for two or three miles, until they reached the abandoned carts and the precious cargo they contained. Returning with as much plunder as they could carry, these spoils were soon distributed among needy comrades, shoes being the most prized of trophies. But the items were not given away freely; rather, they were sold at exorbitant prices on promise of payment at Corunna or Portsmouth; and, as Blakeney observed:

> 'Some of those promissory notes became post-obits next evening along the road to Constantino, and many more shared the same fate before and at the Battle of Corunna. . . '

Despite the signs – evident at Cacabellos – that battle was the best medication for ailing British morale, Moore remained obsessed with hurrying his men forward as fast as possible. On 5 January, he decreed a forced march of thirty-six hours' duration, an order which – considering the cruel weather, the execrable mountain roads, and the precarious state of the army – was bound to provoke a backlash of bitterness and indignation. According to Charles Stewart, this feat, 'was more than men, reduced to the low ebb to which our soldiers had fallen, could endure.' While Adam Neale, an army physician, declared:

> 'All that had hitherto been suffered by our troops was but a prelude to this time of horrors . . . Our men had now become quite mad with despair.'[5]

Certainly for many, like the 'Soldier of the 71st', the real nightmare began with this non-stop slog over the last of the Cantabrian Mountains:

> 'Dreadful as our former march had been, it was from Villafranca that the march of death may be said to have begun . . . There was nothing to sustain our famished bodies or [provide] shelter from the rain or snow. We were either drenched with rain or crackling with ice. Fuel we could find none. The sick and wounded that we had been still enabled to drag with us in wagons were now left to perish in the snow. The road was one line of bloody footmarks from the sore

feet of the men; and on its sides lay the dead and the dying.'

Military pundits have accused Moore ever since of inflicting excessive suffering on his men at this stage of the retreat, by setting a punishing pace when there seemed little need to do so. They point to the facts that his pursuers were almost at their last gasp, that the mountain passes provided numerous defensive positions, and that whenever British troops had clashed with the French, they had been victorious without exception. Stewart – whose account of the campaign is generally critical of Sir John – believed him to be daunted by the responsibilities of command, claiming, furthermore, that 'he *underrated* the qualities of his own troops, and greatly *overrated* those of his adversary.' Though there may be an element of truth in these statements (Moore was undoubtedly acutely aware that he was responsible not just for *a* British army, but *the* British army – the only field army the nation then possessed), Sir Charles Oman was surely nearer the mark in his observation that Sir John, 'shocked at the state of indiscipline into which his regiments were falling, thought only of getting to the sea as quickly as possible.' Whatever Moore's motives, the march between Villafranca and Lugo would test even the toughest veterans, and in the event would claim as many casualties as a pitched battle, as Stewart confirmed:

> 'The horrors of this retreat have been again and again described in terms calculated to freeze the blood of such as read them, but I have no hesitation in saying that the most harrowing accounts which have yet been laid before the public, fall short of the reality.'

Once clear of Herrerias, the route to Corunna turned into a treacherous, tortuous climb over snowbound mountain spurs, before reaching the upland plains of the Lugo plateau beyond. This sixty-mile stretch contained some of the bleakest, most desolate country in Spain. August Schaumann gave a vivid description:

'At every step we took, we waded through snow and mud over the bodies of dead men and horses. The howling wind, as it whistled past the ledges of rock and through the bare trees, sounded to the ear like the groaning of the damned; and while the darkness certainly concealed all the horrors of our plight, it only made us the more attentive to the moans of the dying and the execrations of the hungry.'

These curses fell, for the most part, on the Commissariat, which had consistently failed in its primary task of distributing the army's provisions. This much-maligned branch of the service was composed, not of military men but untrained civilian clerks, who were accountable only to the Treasury Department in London. From the very moment they landed in Spain, these Whitehall warriors had been obliged to contend with uncooperative officials, a shocking degree of poverty and lassitude among the populace, and a chronic lack of transport. Ready cash might have eased the logistical logjam, but although money had been lavished on the Spaniards, London apparently expected Moore to run his campaign on a shoestring, and failed to supply him with sufficient funds. As a consequence, hungry soldiers began to starve and Schaumann describes how men:

'. . .flung themselves down in despair in the midst of the mud and filth on the side of the road. Insubordination was noticeable everywhere . . . and many bitter remarks were made, all of which usually ended with the following prayer: "Give us something to eat; let us just take a little rest, then lead us against the enemy, and we shall beat him!"'

But the soldiers could obtain nothing from their exasperated officers, nor from the impoverished peasants, who, naturally enough, were inclined to keep what little provender they possessed for themselves. French prisoners of war, marching with Moore's columns, were both amused and exasperated by their captors' lack of experience in the harsh realities of campaign life. On one occasion, a French officer volunteered to provide food for his escort and, summoning a village patriarch, knocked the poor man flat before demanding breakfast for the whole party – the rustic soon reappeared with all that was required.

As the troops continued to toil up the mountain tracks like beasts of burden, laden with the equivalent of their own body weight in kit, the order came – to some fortunates like William Green of the 1st Battalion, 95th, at least – to discard their hated knapsacks:

> 'We did not mind parting with our kits so we left them by the roadside. But then we had enough to carry: fifty round of ball cartridge, thirty loose balls in our waist belt and a flask and a horn of powder, and rifle and sword, the two weighing fourteen pounds. These were plenty for us to carry with empty bellies and the enemy close at our heels, thirsting for our blood!'

For others, however, the order to remove knapsacks never arrived, for John Dobbs of the 52nd describes the extraordinary feat of a man in his brother's company, who, though only five feet three inches tall, nevertheless managed to carry both his own knapsack and that of an exhausted comrade who towered above him at almost six feet, 'breadth making up for length'. Encumbered or not, however, the conditions the men endured were cruel, the rate of march gruelling, and according to William Green:

> 'Many of our men sat down by the roadside and gave up the ghost, fairly worn down. Those who could use tobacco held out the best. I was one of this number. We had seven or eight women belonging to the Regiment. There were no baggage wagons on which they could ride and some of them fell into the hands of the enemy; and after using them as they pleased, they gave them some food and sent them to us!'

As previously noted, inexperienced officers, unaware of the hardships to come, had permitted a large number of women to accompany the army at the outset of the campaign. Most of these spouses, common-law wives, and camp followers possessed no official status and were protected by no laws. Many were accompanied by small children and some were even in the advanced stages of pregnancy. Their plight was one of the most tragic aspects of the whole retreat, and in the words of Charles Stewart, these poor creatures:

> '...heightened the horror of passing events, by a display of suffering even more acute than that endured by their husbands. Some were taken in labour on the road; and in the open air, amidst showers of sleet and snow, gave birth to infants which, with their mothers, perished as soon as they had seen light. Others, carrying, some of them, two children on their backs, toiled on, and when they came to look to the condition of their burdens, they would probably find one or both frozen to death.'

Though some wives were actually hardier than their husbands, in general, the suffering of the soldiers' womenfolk was, as Stewart suggests, truly appalling. The 'Soldier of the 71st' describes a particularly distressing tableau which drew a crowd of horrified onlookers on the descent of Monte del Castro:

> 'In the centre lay a woman, young and lovely, though cold in death, and a child, apparently about six or seven months old, attempting to draw support from the breast of its dead mother. Tears filled every eye, but no one had the power to aid. While we stood around, gazing on the interesting object, then on each other, none offered to speak, each heart was so full. At length one of General Moore's staff-officers came up and desired the infant to be given to him. He rolled it in his cloak, amidst the blessings of every spectator. Never shall I efface the benevolence of his look from my heart, when he said, "Unfortunate infant, you will be my future care."'

At daybreak on 5 January, as the leading columns quit Constantino and crawled towards Lugo (and messengers scampered down the Vigo road after the unfortunate General

Fraser), the Reserve prepared to quit Nogales. The troops –
many of whom were now sporting stolen Spanish uniforms
and shoes – had just got clear of the place, when the pursuing
French dragoons made their appearance. As usual, Soult's
horsemen had ridden well in advance of their infantry
supports and, unable to mount a full-scale attack, made do
with prodding Edward Paget's rearguard up the road and over
what Blakeney describes as a 'romantic' bridge. This structure
defied the best efforts of Moore's engineers to destroy it, and
the regiments of the Reserve were obliged to continue their
retreat up a winding road to the summit of a nearby hill. It
was here that Paget proceeded to lay a trap for his pursuers.
Using the guns of his artillery as bait – by leaving them
apparently abandoned on the brow of the hill – Paget formed
up his infantry on the reverse slope, out of sight of the
oncoming enemy, and waited. Although a few intrepid
Frenchmen forded the river and reached the base of Paget's
hill, the bulk of Soult's advanced guard simply gathered on the
opposite bank, and in their turn, also fell to waiting.
Eventually, says Blakeney:

> 'The General merely remarked, "It is no matter," and
> ordered the guns to be horsed, saying, "These fellows
> don't seem inclined to add to their artillery." Had they
> indeed taken the guns, which I believe it was the
> intention of the General to permit, they could never
> have been more warmly received, and they would have
> paid most dearly for their momentarily held prize
> . . . The General, observing our disappointment at the
> reluctance of the enemy to come forward to attack us,
> took a pinch of snuff out of his buff-leather waistcoat
> pocket, and said, "28th, if you don't get fighting
> enough, it is not my fault."'

Paget's men pressed on as rapidly as possible, hugging a
steep and slippery mountain track, bordered by a sheer
precipice. Around noon, having gained a couple of miles on
their enemies, they were permitted to halt and rest for a few
minutes. It was at this point that a certain Mr Courtney of the
Paymaster-General's Department rode back from just ahead,

anxiously seeking Sir Edward. Courtney had been left in
charge of two bullock-carts containing the army's emergency
fund of £25,000 in silver dollars.[6] These carts, after lagging
behind Baird's Division, had eventually come to grief on the
road with the failure of the beasts which drew them.
Schaumann had passed the spot some time earlier, noting that:

> 'The bullocks were lying on the ground under their
> yokes, utterly exhausted. A soldier with bayonet fixed
> stood guard over the treasure, and with a desperate air
> implored every officer that passed by to relieve him of
> his duty.'

Now Courtney, in a state of extreme agitation, was come
to beg General Paget's assistance. His request, and the
response it elicited from an apoplectic Paget, have been
recorded for posterity by Robert Blakeney:

> '"The treasure of the army, sir, is close in the rear, and
> the bullocks being jaded are unable to proceed; I
> therefore want fresh animals to draw it forward."
> "Pray, sir," said the General, "do you take me for a
> bullock-driver or a muleteer, or knowing who I am,
> have you the presence of mind coolly to tell me that
> through a total neglect or ignorance of your duty, you
> are about to lose the treasure of the army committed
> to your charge, which, according to your account, must
> shortly fall into the hands of that enemy?" (And he
> pointed to the French advanced guard, who were
> closing upon us.) "Had you, sir, the slightest conception
> of your duty, you would have known that you ought to
> be a day's march ahead of the whole army, instead of
> hanging back with your foundered bullocks and carts
> upon the rearmost company of the rearguard, and
> making your report too at the very moment when that
> company is absolutely engaged with the advancing
> enemy. What, sir! To come to me and impede my
> march with your carts and ask me to look for bullocks
> when I should be free from all encumbrances and my
> mind occupied by no other care than that of disposing
> my troops to the best advantage in resisting the

approaching enemy! It is doubtful, sir, whether your conduct can be attributed to ignorance and neglect alone." There were other expressions equally strong which are now in part forgotten; yet the words, "Ought to be hanged!" have remained hanging on my memory for many years.'

In the meantime, the French advanced guard had been steadily gaining ground, and their musket balls were now falling among the British troops. Paget kept Courtney under fire long enough 'to show him the different use of silver and lead during a campaign,'[7] before beating a hasty retreat, only to bump into the Paymaster's stranded silver. Finding the carts completely immovable, and with the enemy at his heels, Paget ordered the casks containing the coins to be stoved in and rolled over the cliff face. Lieutenant Bennet of the 28th was entrusted with this task and given additional orders to shoot any man who tried to help himself to the loot. In Charles Stewart's view, however, this sacrifice of army cash:

'... was an unwise and also a useless measure. Had it been distributed among the soldiers, there is little doubt that they would have contrived to carry it along; whereas, the knowledge that it lay among the cliffs, tempted many men to lag behind, who fell into the hands of the enemy or perished from cold.'

These stragglers were not the only ones who risked death or capture for a fistful of dollars, for several women joined in the treasure hunt and, according to some accounts, the wife of the 52nd's master tailor – one Mrs Maloney – managed to stash away a small fortune in her clothing. And so, too, did the wife of a certain Corporal Bailey of the 42nd, but with tragic consequences. Anthony Hamilton tells how the ill-fated female:

'... so loaded herself with the money that was scattered about, that afterwards, when embarking in Corunna harbour, in trying to get up into the vessel, she had such a weight around her person, that she fell between the boat and ship and was drowned.'

The bulk of the abandoned wealth, however, despite the efforts of malingerers, matrons and sharp-eyed French dragoons, fell into the hands of jubilant Spanish peasants with the coming of the spring thaw.

In the late afternoon Paget's Reserve Division, accompanied by Moore himself, breasted the hill overlooking the bridge of Constantino and the village beyond. Sir John was loathe to give up this commanding position to the French before his troops had completed their descent of the hill's reverse slope, and crossed the bridge at its base to safety. He placed his guns on the summit of the hill, therefore, and, leaving the 95th to protect them, hurried his remaining regiments forward. The French, however, merely halted on an opposite hill and proceeded to waste half an hour gawping at the British guns and riflemen. This gave the redcoats time to get safely across the river and Moore ordered his artillery and its escort to retire. This movement was the signal for a renewed French advance and Lahoussaye's cavalry – now supported by Merle's infantry – poured down from their perch into the valley below.

The British rearguard, however, had been permitted to prepare an appropriate reception for them. The guns, having rejoined their division, were trained on the bridge; the 95th and 28th Regiments were extended along the bank of the river; and the remaining regiments of the Reserve – the 20th, 52nd, and 91st – were all formed up, under Sir John Moore's personal supervision, on a nearby ridge. According to Charles Stewart:

> 'The enemy came on with apparent boldness. His cavalry and *tirailleurs* attempted to pass the bridge: but they were met, not only by the fire of the riflemen, but by a heavy and well-directed cannonade from the high grounds. They were driven back; but in a few moments they renewed their efforts, and with a similar want of success; and again, after a short pause, the attempt was made a third time. Darkness put an end to the skirmish, and they withdrew.'

Though the French lost as many as 300 men killed and wounded at Constantino, British losses were minimal and at 11.00 p. m. the Reserve continued its march unmolested.

Twenty miles up the Corunna road, the men of Moore's vanguard had been trickling into the wretched little town of Lugo all day. They were at the extremes of hunger and exhaustion, and much of their baggage and equipment had been lost or abandoned. According to Captain Gordon:

> 'All the straggling and irregularities that had occurred on any former occasion might be considered as the perfection of discipline if compared with the retreat from Villafranca, which resembled the flight of an indisciplined rabble rather than the march of regular troops; and a comparison at this period betwixt the British army and Romana's mob would not have been much in favour of the former.'

And so the retreat from Villafranca to Lugo – the 'march of death' – was almost over. It is difficult to be precise with regard to losses along the way, for many men who were presumed missing or dead made their appearance over the next few days, straggling into Lugo to rejoin the colours. Sir Charles Oman, however, claims that approximately 2,000 troops were lost on the road between Astorga and Lugo, and it is reasonable to assume that the bulk of these casualties occurred after Villafranca.

As for the bodies of the dead, there was insufficient time and resources to afford them interment. The 'Soldier of the 71st' describes how the corpses of women and children, frozen to death, were taken down from the few remaining wagons to be laid out on the snow, 'An old tattered blanket, or some other piece of garment, was all the burial that was given them.' As for the fallen soldiers, they lay:

> '. . . uncovered until the next fall of snow, or heavy drift, concealed their bodies . . . Amidst scenes like these, we arrived at Lugo.'

Notes

1. The name given to punishment by fire, a sentence favoured by the Spanish Inquisition.
2. Napier, *History of the War in the Peninsula.*
3. There were three Napier brothers serving in the Corunna Campaign, all of them devoted followers of Moore: Charles James (1782–1853) was the eldest and was a major in the 50th Regiment; George Thomas (1784–1855) was the second and was a captain and aide on Moore's staff; William Francis (1785–1860) was a captain in the 43rd Regiment. All three men were remarkable soldiers and went on to carve out glittering careers: Charles became one of Britain's greatest generals and military heroes of the 19th century; George became Governor of the Cape; and William – according to some the most handsome man of his day – became an outstanding author and historian, his *History of the War in the Peninsula and in the South of France, From the Year 1807 to the Year 1814*, being the consummate study of the conflict.
4. A deliberate murder.
5. Neale, *The Spanish Campaign of 1808.*
6. Over £1,000,000 in modern reckoning.
7. Blakeney, *A Boy in the Peninsular War.*

CHAPTER 9

The Stragglers' Battle

At 10.00 a. m. on 6 January, Moore arrived at Lugo with the Reserve to find the rest of the army already assembled. Sir John, it seems, was horrified at the disorganised, ramshackle state of his leading divisions, and the apparent losses which they had sustained on the march from Villafranca: 'Soldiers,' he declared, 'if you do not behave better, I would rather be a shoe-black than your general.' Most of Moore's ire, however, was thrown at his regimental officers in a scathing General Order, in which he expressed his exasperation at 'the complete disorganisation of the army', and his weariness with 'giving orders which were never attended to'. Under all the circumstances, these words were harsh, especially as many soldiers were by now so cowed by suffering, that death – never mind discipline – no longer intimidated them. Thus, Captain Gordon no doubt spoke for many an aggrieved subaltern, when he observed that:

> '. . . it was not possible for the officers, who encountered the same hardships and privations, to superintend the conduct of their men in the manner they are accustomed to do in barracks or quarters in England.'

For their part, the officers of the vanguard blamed Moore for pushing them too hard, while remaining oblivious to their plight by constantly accompanying the Reserve.

Moore's mood, however, gradually improved as he realised he had the following assets: firstly, sufficient food stores existed at Lugo to sustain his army for a few days at least; secondly, reinforcements had been found in the form of Leith's Brigade, a unit left behind by Baird when he first advanced from Astorga, and which, as a consequence, had been retreating at a leisurely pace ahead of the main column. Now, at Lugo, this relatively fresh brigade – consisting of some 1,800 men – was reunited with the army, bringing its strength back up to about 19,000 effectives. Thirdly, hundreds of men who had fallen behind on the march and been given up for lost, made a happy appearance, hobbling into Lugo throughout the morning, determined to rejoin their colours for the coming battle. Finally, the spot which Moore had selected to stop Soult – though described by General Charles Stewart as 'a tolerably advantageous position, along the summit of a range of low hills' – was, in fact, virtually impregnable. Lying three or four miles in advance of the town, its right wing rested on the unfordable River Miño, while its left was anchored on a range of rocky and inaccessible hills. This formidable position was further strengthened by a network of walls and hedges in its front – boundary markers for fields and vineyards – which acted as a kind of obstacle course for any would-be attacker.

According to James Moore, Sir John, 'had received certain intelligence that three divisions of the French army were now in his front; which, though a force considerably superior to his own, he wished to engage.' In truth, however, Soult's force was now no stronger than Moore's – possibly even weaker, if French sources are to be believed[1] – and in a similar state of disarray. Many French troops had fallen out from fatigue and hunger, and taken to marauding roadside villages, while one whole infantry division, that of Heudelet, was still kicking its heels at Villafranca. Thus, when the marshal arrived before the British battle-line at noon, accompanied by Merle's infantry and the cavalry of Franceschi and Lahoussaye, he felt no inclination to commit himself. His coyness was enhanced by the fact that, due to the nature of the ground, it was almost impossible to perceive the strength of the force facing him.

Unsure whether he had Moore's whole army before him or merely its rearguard, Soult opted to wait on events, while requesting Ney to make haste with the 20,000 troops of VI Corps.

As for Moore, believing himself to be outnumbered, he had little choice but to stay put in his rocky fortress and prepare to be attacked. He made good use of the hiatus, by reorganising and re-equipping his divisions, and forwarding the few remaining women with the baggage to Corunna. Meanwhile, Captain Gordon noted that:

> 'Many of the inhabitants did not appear to bear us much goodwill. Most of the shops were shut up, and business of all kind was at a standstill; provisions were scarce, but the troops received biscuit, rum, and salt beef, from the sea-stores, which had been ordered to meet us here. A great number of horses and mules that were lame, or in other respects unfit for service, were shot, and the streets and roads near the city were much obstructed by their carcasses.'

Thus the day passed calmly enough; and for the British, at least, in quiet anticipation of a coming storm.

Next morning, Sir John made the following announcement:

> 'The army must see that the moment is now come, when, after the hardships and fatiguing marches they have undergone, they will have the opportunity of bringing the enemy to action. The Commander of the Forces has the most perfect confidence in their valour, and that it is only necessary to bring them to close contact with the enemy in order to defeat them; and a defeat, if it be complete, as he trusts it will be, will, in a great measure, end their labours ... The General has no other caution to give them, than not to throw away their fire at the enemy's skirmishers, merely because they fire at them; but to reserve it till they can give it with effect.'

At last, the moment Moore's men had longed for was at hand: a trial by battle in which, they doubted not, they would emerge victorious. The effect which Sir John's notification of imminent combat had upon his regiments was remarkable. Morale lifted, discipline returned, and despite an incessant downpour, the troops turned out at break of day:

> '...as clean as if we had just come out of our barrack-
> room in Colchester, and marched as orderly into
> position in front of Lugo as if crossing a parade ground
> in England.'[2]

In the French camp, Soult had been joined by the infantry divisions of Mermet and Delaborde, as well as the cavalry of Lorges. Nevertheless, the marshal was still fretting over the number of redcoats ranged before him and at some point that morning – Stewart says 'scarcely after dawn', Gordon 'about eleven o'clock', while Napier hints at noon – he sent forward four artillery pieces, under a cavalry escort, in order to test the British line. No sooner had the cannonade begun, however, when it was silenced by the furious fire of fifteen British guns. Soult, now knew that he faced more than a mere rearguard. Warily, he proceeded to probe the British position further. A feint was made against Moore's right wing, which was intended to mask a more serious effort upon his left by Merle's infantry. The former blow was beaten off without much trouble by Warde's Foot Guards; while the latter was repulsed by Leith's Brigade in a bayonet-charge which claimed 300 French casualties.

As it happened, these assaults were made while Moore was reconnoitring, accompanied by his staff and a lady on a white charger, who turned out to be the wife of Colonel MacKenzie of the 5th Regiment: 'She betrayed no signs of uneasiness,' noticed Gordon, 'although the enemy sent a few balls at the party.' As soon as Sir John saw that the main French effort was directed against his left, he dashed to the scene of action, rallying his men and exhorting them to see off their assailants with cold steel. According to James Moore, Sir John found himself in the midst of the 51st and 76th Regiments:

> 'He addressed them in an animated tone and
> commanded them to advance: when the Light

Company of the 76th rushed forward with charged bayonets and drove the enemy down the hill with considerable loss ... In this sharp skirmish Captain Roberts of the 51st was shot in the hand, but before the Frenchman could recover his musket he was transfixed by a soldier of the 76th named Canner. This brave fellow bayoneted two other Frenchmen and was rewarded by promotion.'

Battle having at last been joined, the British, Gordon declared, were eager to finish the business:

'From the first moment of the attack and as long as the French were before us discipline was restored, and the officers were as punctually obeyed as if we had been on parade at home. We felt not our sufferings, so anxious were we to end them by a victory, which we were certain of obtaining.'

But Soult was unwilling to oblige. His half-hearted sallies having been repulsed in the most spirited and violent manner, he judged himself sufficiently well informed as to his enemy's strength, and withdrew from the field. Thus, with the fall of dusk, the fatigued and frustrated redcoats – having spent the entire day formed up for battle – were stood down and sent back to their billets, 'with the fervent wish that the dawn of morning might light them to battle.'[3]

For many, however, the bitter cold night was spent out in the open, ready to repel the French offensive which, it was hoped, must surely arrive with the dawn. The 'Private of the 42nd' remembered how his battalion suffered:

'We took up our position in close column that night. The night being very cold, we collected all the wood we could find to keep on large fires. I was very unwell that night, and wrapping myself up in my greatcoat I lay by the fire. Our officers, poor fellows, sat by us, roasting potatoes all night; folks say, "like master like man," it was like man like officer here. Hunger, like death, is a ruthless leveller.'

As for the 'Soldier of the 71st' and his comrades, they spent the night on their feet in a freezing field, arms piled, longing for a fight to put them out of their misery:

> 'The sky was one continued expanse of stars; not a cloud to be seen, and the frost was most intense. Words fail me to express what we suffered from the most dreadful cold. We alternately went to the calm side of each other, to be sheltered from the wind. In this manner, when day at length broke upon us, we had retrograded over two fields from the spot where we had piled our arms. Many had lain down, through the night, overcome by sleep, from which the last trumpet only will awaken them.'

Early next morning, 8 January, Sir John assembled his troops once more and, riding through the ranks, 'had the pleasure of finding that, in consequence of the orders he had issued, of the exertions of the officers, and above all, of the hopes of an action, regularity was restored.'[4] The soldiers, worn down by the attacks of deadly, yet intangible enemies such as hunger, cold and fatigue, now craved a chance to contend with foes of flesh and blood. According to Stewart, Moore, too, was anxious to fight, before Lugo's food ran out or the French were reinforced:

> 'Sir John ...no longer entertained a doubt that the hour of trial was at hand. He sincerely rejoiced in the conviction; for the prospect of a battle had restored to the army the whole of its confidence and much of its discipline; and the General saw that it was only by beating his pursuers – and beating them effectually – that he could free himself from their presence, and secure orderly embarkation.'

But Soult steadfastly refused to bestir himself and, as the hours slipped through Moore's fingers, despondency returned to the British camp, with the realisation that they were to be defeated not by force, but by time. Captain Gordon was one of those who waited in vain for the action to begin:

'We passed the day in a state of anxious suspense, impatiently listening for the roar of artillery, which we expected to mark the commencement of the action; and as hour after hour elapsed without any demonstration on either side, a universal feeling of the most bitter disappointment spread through the ranks.'

Any aggressive movement on the part of the British was ruled out, as Stewart explains, 'because the French were understood to exceed us in numbers, and they occupied ground difficult of approach, with every facility for retreating.' In fact, with food stocks running low and little remaining transport for the conveyance of ammunition, supplies, the sick and the wounded, Moore could hardly be expected to take the offensive. Even if he had done so, and managed to defeat Soult – whose position was as formidable as his own – he would simply have stumbled into Marshal Ney's VI Corps, with catastrophic results.

The hopelessness of the situation hit Moore hard. He had made a stand at Lugo in the expectation of being attacked; but Soult, the wily 'Duke of Damnation', held the initiative and wielded that most merciless of all weapons: time. Sir John realised that he had nothing to gain by lingering at Lugo and at midnight, after the destruction of the remaining stores and 500 crippled horses, ordered his army back onto the Corunna road: 'We marched all night,' recollected Stewart, 'both men and horses suffering dreadfully from cold, fatigue and hunger.' Meanwhile, the troopers of Sir Richard Hussey Vivian's 7th Hussars remained behind on rearguard duty, stoking the huge fires which had been left burning along the abandoned British line, in order to fool the French.

But Soult could see nothing; the night was as black as pitch, and a continuous downpour of rain reduced visibility even further. These atrocious conditions, however, which helped confound the French, also blinded the British and Moore's plans for a quick getaway went sadly awry. The rain turned into an icy, stinging sleet, forcing forlorn soldiers to ferret out shelter, and a ferocious wind blew up, extinguishing lamps, and sapping the energy of those who attempted to march.

Meanwhile, whole brigades were thrown into chaos, as the guides employed to lead them blundered in the dark, amid a maze of walls, hedges, vineyards, and lanes. As dawn approached, the army had barely moved five miles, instead of the fifteen Moore had bargained for. Only the Reserve Division had reached its appointed place in the line of march, while the remaining regiments lay scattered across the countryside, still struggling to get their bearings. Soult, however, slept on, and the redcoats – aided by the rays of a bleary winter sun – eventually made good their escape.

At 5.00 on the morning of the 9th, the 7th Hussars quit their post and followed the scattered columns *en route* for Corunna via Betanzos. Sir Richard Hussey Vivian recorded the scene:

> 'Although I left the advanced posts . . . full four hours after the retreat of our army, I found the houses on the outskirts of the town full of stragglers. Many of these I succeeded in driving out by force or persuasion. Others were so ill and harassed that nothing could move them . . . Every house was full (I may say, out of some we drove upwards of 100) of these stragglers, and such was the state of carelessness and the total want of spirit occasioned by fatigue, etc., that on being told that the enemy would certainly shoot them, many replied, "They may shoot us, sir, as you may shoot us, but we cannot stir."'

Many bone-weary men took to hiding in bundles of straw, the exasperated hussars being obliged to prod them out with the points of their swords before pushing them forward up the road. 'It was a most fatiguing march,' recorded Sir John Slade, 'as we did not go above two miles an hour, being obliged to regulate our pace by the infantry, and it rained for thirty-six hours.' Indeed, the road presented a sorry sight, and Hussey Vivian tells of:

> 'Fine fellows, willing and anxious to get on, their feet bleeding for want of shoes, and totally incapable of keeping up; others, whose spirit was better than their

strength, actually striving till the last to join their battalions, and several of this description perished in the attempt . . . every now and then you met with a poor unfortunate woman, perhaps with a child in her arms, without shoes or stockings, knee deep in mud, crying most piteously for that assistance which, alas, we could not afford her.'

In spite of Moore's best efforts, most of the women continued to lag behind, suffering the most cruel and wretched conditions without help or succour. Many succumbed to death on the road, and in a particularly horrific example, Schaumann describes how one poor woman sank:

'. . . up to her waist in a bog, whereupon, the mud and slime preventing her from rising, she fell, and the whole column marched over her.'

By mid-morning, Marshal Soult had woken up to the fact that the British had walked. Cautiously entering Lugo, he found the place deserted of troops but piled high with broken equipment, spoiled food, and dead horses. The marshal immediately despatched Franceschi's cavalry in hot pursuit, but Moore had stolen almost half a day's march and was already across the Miño, leaving behind a team of Royal Engineers, but with wet powder and virtually no sappers or equipment, to destroy the bridge at Rabade. Gordon saw how difficult this proved to be:

'The stream is broad and rapid, the bank rotten, and the neighbourhood does not furnish material for making even a temporary repair. The destruction of this bridge was therefore expected to throw considerable impediments in the way of the enemy's advance; but our hopes were again disappointed. The powder exploded, the bridge remained uninjured, and the French crossed the river within a few hours after us. . . '

Nevertheless, the condition of the troops – many of whom had been marching for at least twelve hours – compelled a halt, which according to Charles Stewart, was relished 'under a pelting rain, and totally devoid of shelter.'

Meanwhile, the 15th Hussars entered the village of Guitiriz in the midst of what Captain Gordon describes as, 'the most violent storm of hail and rain I ever witnessed.' While the men rested as best they could in the open, Gordon and his brother officers squeezed into the kitchen of a large house, occupied by Sir David Baird and his staff:

> 'I had been so fortunate as to obtain a place near the fire, round which a number of officers and men of different corps were assembled to dry their clothes and thaw their half-frozen limbs; but we were soon disturbed by Sir David Baird's cook, who insisted upon having the fire entirely to herself, that she might boil his tea-kettle. She was so violently enraged at our non-compliance with this unreasonable demand that, after scolding herself out of breath, she retired in great dudgeon ... In a few minutes an *aide-de-camp* appeared, who informed us that Sir David Baird desired we would all quit his house, which had been allotted for his quarters. However excusable such a stretch of authority might have been in ordinary circumstances, we felt that in our situation it was carrying the privileges of military rank too far, and no one seemed inclined to exchange the comparative comfort of the place we occupied for a bivouac in the open street, exposed to the pelting of the storm, merely to gratify the spleen of Sir David's cook. Brigadier-General Fane, who was one of the party, remonstrated with the *aide-de-camp* on the harshness and indelicacy of sending such a message to a number of officers and he, who seemed uncomfortable at being obliged to deliver it, quitted the room without insisting on our departure.'

Moore, meanwhile, was desperately concerned about the column's lack of progress, and the 2,000-strong army of stragglers dawdling along in its rear:

> 'It is evident that the enemy will not fight this army, notwithstanding the superiority of his numbers; but will

endeavour to harass and tease it upon its march
... The Commander of the Forces requests that it may
be carefully explained to the soldiers, that their safety
depends solely upon their keeping their divisions, and
marching with their regiments; that those who stop in
villages, or straggle on the march, will inevitably be cut
off by the French cavalry; who have hitherto shown
little mercy even to the feeble and infirm, who have
fallen into their hands ... The army has still eleven
leagues to march, the soldiers must make an exertion
to accomplish them; the rearguard cannot stop, and
those who fall behind must take their fate.'

And yet the rearguard did stop, as Robert Blakeney
testifies, to round up and drive forward those who forsook
their colours:

'Some of the divisions in front, instead of keeping
together on the road during a halt, which took place
on the approach of the night of the 9th, were permitted
to separate and go into buildings; and on their divisions
marching off, immense numbers were left behind, so
that when the Reserve came up we were halted to
rouse up the stragglers. In many instances we
succeeded, but generally failed; we kicked, thumped,
struck with the butt ends of the firelocks, pricked with
swords and bayonets, but to little purpose.'

The army was now a mere sixty miles or so from Corunna,
yet the soldiers' burden of suffering was such, that many, like
the 'Private of the 42nd', cared little:

'I was now quite careless about my fate. I heeded not
man; I cared not if I fell into the hands of the French;
I was harassed out of my very life. Still I continued on
the line of march with the regiment for four hours.
Sleep at length overcame me, and I would be
marching and sleeping, literally walking asleep, till I
would come bump against the man in front of me. I
often thought that if I could get a convenient place, I
would lie down and take a nap, let the consequences
be what they might. By this time there were not 300

men with the regiment out of 1,000 who entered Spain:
many had fallen a sacrifice to the hardships of fatigue,
hunger, and disease, on the line of march, and many
more had been taken or massacred by the French, who
pursued us. As we plodded on, some haystacks
presented themselves to our view, and I resolved to
repose a little. I was not many minutes down, when I
felt so cold and stiff that I could not sleep. I got up
again, but my feet were very sore, as if I were walking
on a card for wool. I made up to the regiment in the
course of an hour: it was like getting to my father's
door, to join my comrades once more.'

Hunger, fatigue, cold, sickness – none of these afflictions
were respecters of rank or privilege; and many took a perverse
pleasure in seeing their social superiors reduced to the same
sorry state as themselves: 'The officers, in many points,
suffered as much as the men,' noted the 'Soldier of the 71st':

'I have seen officers of the Guards, and others worth
thousands, with pieces of old blankets wrapt round
their feet and legs; the men pointing at them, with a
malicious satisfaction, saying, "There goes three
thousand a year"; or "There goes the prodigal son on
his return to his father, cured of his wanderings." Even
in the midst of all our sorrows, there was a bitterness
of spirit, a savageness of wit, that made a jest of its own
miseries.'

Thus the march continued during the night of 9–10
January, with straggling, indiscipline, and plundering
plumbing new depths. The Galician peasants, terrified of the
French invader, had abandoned their homes *en masse* and fled
to the hills; the British troops, made churlish by deprivation
and distress, mistook their flight for betrayal, and proceeded to
ransack their homes in revenge.[5] In their defence, it might be
added that many, by this stage, were almost mad with hunger,
and, according to Captain Gordon:

'Straggling had increased to such a degree that, if the
retreat had continued three days longer, the army must

have been totally annihilated. The men were so much exhausted by incessant fatigue and want of food, added to the effects of a violent dysentery which raged amongst them, that many who lay down to rest themselves at a little distance from the roadside had not sufficient strength to rejoin the line of march and fell into the hands of the enemy.'

By mid-afternoon on 10 January, Moore's leading elements began to file into Betanzos in the most deplorable state imaginable. According to the 'Private of the 42nd':

'All that came in of our regiment were 150 men. We had not an officer to carry the colours; all fell behind ... This shows what the retreat to Corunna was. I have not language to express what hardships I endured; and if I were to tell you all the men said of this retreat, you would think I had fabricated libels on the memory of Sir John Moore.'

Meanwhile, outside the town, the Reserve halted on a range of hills to cover the thousands of stragglers pouring in from the rear. From this vantage point they witnessed a curious incident, which came to be known as the Stragglers' Battle.

Franceschi's cavalry, having bagged some 500 prisoners on the road, arrived before a village where these stragglers were assembling. From instinct, the desperadoes formed up across the road into a solid mass and began firing upon the French. A sergeant of the 43rd assumed command and, dividing his force into two groups, proceeded to leapfrog them up the road to Betanzos, each section taking its turn to face the enemy, while the other pushed on. Robert Blakeney described how his seniors viewed the incident:

'General Paget saw the whole affair, and perceiving that they were capable of defending themselves, deemed it unnecessary to send them any support; but he declared in presence of the men, who from a natural impulse wished to move down against the cavalry, that his reason for withholding support was that he would not sacrifice the life of one good soldier who had stuck to his colours to save the whole horde of drunken marauders who by their disgraceful conduct placed themselves at the mercy of their enemies.'

Having successfully escaped their pursuers, the stragglers were soon secured by Paget, who sent a strong picket to prod them forward into Betanzos. There each man had his haversack removed and searched for plunder, and as Blakeney describes:

> '. . . all the money found upon them, which it was fully ascertained could have been acquired by robbery only, was collected in a heap and distributed among the men who never swerved from their colours, thus rewarding the meritorious and well disciplined, to the mortification of those who disgraced their profession . . . But it is totally impossible to enumerate the different articles of plunder which they contrived to cram into their packs and haversacks. Brass candlesticks bent double, bundles of common knives, copper saucepans hammered into masses, every sort of domestic utensil which could be forced into their packs, were found upon them without any regard as to value or weight; and the greater number carried double the weight imposed by military regulations or necessity . . . the great body were sent under escort to Betanzos, there to be dealt with by their various corps.'

Notes

1. According to Oman, 'French accounts say that the three
   infantry divisions had only 13,000 bayonets with the eagles,
   instead of the 20,000 whom they should have shown, and
   that the cavalry instead of 6,000 sabres mustered only 4,000.'
2. Blakeney, Robert, *A Boy in the Peninsular War.*
3. Hamilton, *Hamilton's Campaign with Moore and Wellington.*
4. Moore, *Narrative of the Campaign of the British Army in Spain.*
5. According to Oman, 'the good spirit of the Galicians was
   displayed in many places by the way in which they fed
   stragglers, and saved them from the French by showing
   them bypaths over the hills. No less than 500 men who had
   lost their way were passed from village to village by the
   peasants, till they reached Portugal.'

CHAPTER 10

Thank God!
We Are Now Safe!

Moore had lost around 1,000 men on the road from Lugo, due to fatigue, cold, and capture. At Betanzos, however, the troops found sanctuary, if not perhaps complete rest, as August Schaumann recalled:

> 'We slept like drunkards. I was constantly dreaming that I was still riding along the edge of terrible precipices and over rocky heights, and every other minute I would jump into the air with fright, as if in the delirium of fever, constantly imagining that I heard the bugles of the rearguard.'

Fortunately for Schaumann, he was permitted to sleep on, for Moore had decreed that the remainder of 10 January be given up to rest, in order to give the stragglers a chance to rejoin their units. Next day they would march into Corunna and – so they believed – the welcoming arms of the Royal Navy. On this latter point, however, they would be disappointed; for while the soldiers' spirits soared, Sir John's sank with the secret intelligence that, due to contrary winds, the fleet had not yet rounded Cape Finisterre from Vigo, and was still beating about in the Atlantic. No ships, therefore, would be waiting for the army when it marched into port, but rather, a final face-off with the Duke of Damnation.

Having destroyed most of the food and *matériel* at Betanzos (including five guns and thousands of muskets intended for Romana's army, which were dumped in the river), Moore assembled his force before dawn on the 11th, for the final march of the campaign. Refreshed, somewhat, by the interlude at Betanzos, and still blissfully unaware that the Navy was behindhand, the troops prepared for the twenty-mile hike to Corunna in good spirits. All, that is, except a soaking wet, sour-faced Sir John Slade, who sat at the head of the Hussar Brigade, looking, according to Captain Gordon:

> '... very disconsolate, in consequence, as I understood, of the harsh and unjustifiable manner in which he had been treated by Lord Paget under the following circumstances: on our arrival at Betanzos, General Slade, on the plea of indisposition, obtained leave from Sir John Moore to proceed to Corunna, and having established himself in comfortable quarters, took a dose of calomel and retired to bed. When Lord Paget – who had quitted the army some days before in consequence of an attack of ophthalmia – was informed of the General's arrival, he sent him a peremptory order to return to his brigade without a moment's delay; and forced him to set out at night, in a soaking rain, regardless of his pathetic remonstrances and intestinal motions!'

Meanwhile, Moore:

> '...passed every regiment and addressed the commanding officer of each; observing to them, that there was no particular post for a commanding officer, who ought to range on the front, flank, and rear of his regiment; that his eye should be everywhere; and that all straggling should be prevented by the activity of the officers.'[1]

Having rammed this particular homily home, for the last time, Sir John galloped off to reconnoitre the environs of Corunna, and the army was at last set in motion: the main column, as usual, followed by the Reserve; and the Reserve –

again as usual – 'closely attended by Soult's advanced guard, headed by Franceschi's light cavalry.'[2]

Once clear of the town, the troops passed over a bridge which a party of Engineers was about to blast with two kegs of powder. General Paget took the precaution of halting the 28th Regiment to secure the bridge till the work of destruction could be completed. Among these sentinels was Ensign Robert Blakeney, who witnessed the operation's less-than-satisfactory sequel:

> 'The desired explosion now took place by which it was confidently expected that for a short time at least we should be separated from our teasing pursuers, and thus be enabled to arrive in good order before Corunna. Our expectations were, however, blasted by the explosion itself; for as soon as the rubbish had fallen down and the smoke cleared away, to our great surprise and annoyance we perceived that one half of one arch only had been destroyed, the other half and one of the battlements remaining firm.'

In order to buy time for the Engineers to complete the job by keeping the French at bay, Paget sent Blakeney and the Light Company, supported by grenadiers, scrambling back over the semi-demolished arch of the bridge – dubbed 'The Devil's Neck' by the men. The troops had barely touched the opposite bank, however, when they were charged by enemy horsemen, howling for British blood. In an instant, Blakeney was attacked by an officer of dragoons:

> 'I cut at him, but my sword approached no nearer perhaps than his horse's nose; in fact my little light infantry sabre was a useless weapon opposed to an immense mounted dragoon, covered, horse and all, with a large green cloak, which in itself formed a sufficient shield. After the failure of my attack I held my sword horizontally over my head, awaiting the dragoon's blow ... At this very critical moment a man of the company, named Oats, cried out, "Mr Blakeney, we've spun him!" And at the same instant the dragoon fell dead at my feet.'

The remaining Frenchmen were fended off with bayonets till a deadly volley from the grenadiers sent them flying back to Betanzos.

Meanwhile, much to their chagrin, the Engineers had been forced to concede defeat, Spanish masonry proving – once again – more than a match for British powder. Yet, if the army was to reach Corunna unmolested, it was imperative that the crossing be held. Consequently, Paget ordered the 28th to remain at their post, forming, in Blakeney's words, 'a barrier of steel', to thwart the French. In due course, the defiant British picket observed the dark brown columns of General Merle's infantry pour into Betanzos, and prepared to sell their lives dearly. Their enemies, however, declined to negotiate 'The Devil's Neck' and, after a few tense hours, Paget commanded Blakeney and the 28th to quit the bridge and rejoin the line of march:

> '...scarcely had we retired ten minutes when the enemy's advanced guard passed over in polite attendance, maintaining their courteous distance.'

By mid-afternoon, the leading elements of Moore's force finally came within sight of the sea. Schaumann described the relief that many felt:

> 'How my heart leapt for joy when, standing upon a height, I beheld a strip of the blue sea upon the horizon, and, about a mile this side of Corunna descried the masts of a few ships! "Thank God! We are now safe!" I cried, and everybody about me heartily agreed.'

Including, apparently, the 'Private of the 42nd', who recollected that:

> 'When we came in sight of the sea we fancied all was well. When I saw the vessels in the harbour, I was so rejoiced, that in a few hours I was a new man again. What is man made of that he can endure all this? How comes he to adapt himself to such mysterious fortune? These and many other reflections crowded on my

mind at the sight of the salt sea. We had toiled to reach
it, and its stormy bosom gave us joy. Hannibal's men,
I had read at school, were spurred on by the
recollection that the sea was behind them, and that if
they retreated to it they must inevitably perish; we
advanced by the thought that if we could but reach it,
our salvation was sure. . . '

As they approached the bridge at El-Burgo, a mere four
miles from Corunna, the men recovered their discipline and
forgot their hardships: 'I felt all my former despondency drop
from my mind,' wrote the 'Soldier of the 71st', 'My galled feet
trod lighter on the icy road. Every face near me seemed to
brighten up.'

On the opposite bank waited Sir John Moore, judging each
regiment's fitness by the regularity of its march, and preparing
words of praise or condemnation for their commanding
officers, as appropriate. At 3.00 p. m. the Brigade of Guards
appeared, led by a staff-twirling drum-major. Behind him,
marching in perfect step to the beat of their drums, came the
soldiers, formed in column of sections: 'These must be the
Guards,' enthused Sir John.

The people of Corunna, however, were inspired with
nothing but pity at the sight of Moore's army. In fact, so
shocked and appalled were they at this procession of spectres
– men hollowed out by hardship; men tormented by dysentery
or sickening wounds; men who, shoeless, shuffled towards
them on bloody feet, bound in blankets like beggars – that
they made the sign of the cross as the soldiers passed.

As for the troops, their dreams of salvation had to be
postponed when, on closer inspection, Corunna's harbour was
found to contain nothing more than a handful of fishing and
storage vessels. Some, like the 'Soldier of the 71st', shrugged
their shoulders, assuming that the Navy would arrive at any
moment: 'We were not cast down at there being no transports
or ships of war . . . they were hourly expected.' Others, like
the 'Private of the 42nd', were under the impression 'that the
army should be embarked next day.' Captain Gordon,
however, was finally undeceived, when he had 'the

mortification of hearing from naval officers that there was little probability of the fleet we expected arriving for several days.' As this unwelcome news sank in, so did the realisation that there would be no embarkation without a fight.

With typical British phlegm, however, Moore's men made the best of the situation: at least they were off the mountains, the coastal climate was relatively mild, and Corunna was crammed with stores. For some lucky souls – like Commissariat man, August Schaumann – reaching Corunna was tantamount to rediscovering the comforts and joys of civilisation:

> 'I was given a billet in that part of the town known as the Citadel, where I had to ride through another gate, and was quartered in the house of a wealthy gentleman called Don Bernardo Mascoso. We were led into a beautifully furnished sitting-room, which seemed to us like heaven; then we were shown another charming little room with two beds, and were given a glorious meal. Feeling very happy I smoked a few cigars and drank mulled wine with Falludo[3] and went early to bed.'

For others less fortunate – such as the 'Private of the 42nd' – it was a return to monastical austerity: 'I hoped this might be the last time in my life that I slept in the mansion of monks.'

And for the Reserve? It was pretty much business as usual. For when they reached the bridge at El-Burgo on the evening of the 11th, they were immediately halted and obliged to witness yet another demolition job; only this time – as Robert Blakeney recounts – the Engineers were taking no chances:

> 'Extraordinary measures seemed to have been taken for the destruction of the bridge which there crossed the Mero. The preparations being terminated, the 28th Light Company, who still formed the rearguard, crossing over the bridge were drawn up close in its rear. Many remonstrated against our nearness, but were sneeringly assured of being more than safe: thus

high-bred scientific theory scorned the vulgarity of common sense. The explosion at length took place, and completely destroyed two arches; large blocks of masonry whizzed awfully over our heads, and caused what the whole of Soult's cavalry could not effect during the retreat. The Light Company of the 28th and Captain Cameron's company of the 95th broke their ranks and ran like turkeys, and regardless of their bodies crammed their heads into any hole which promised security. The upshot masonic masses continuing their parabolic courses passed far to our rear and becoming independent of the impetus by which they had been disturbed, descended and were deeply buried in the earth. One man of the 28th was killed, and four others severely wounded were sent that night into Corunna. This was the only bridge destroyed during the whole retreat, except that of Castrogonzalo, although many were attempted.'

The Reserve remained at El-Burgo to guard the crossing and foil any attempt by the French to effect repairs. Soldiers from the 28th and 95th Regiments took possession of deserted houses close to the wreck of the bridge, their outlying pickets extended along the riverbank, as Private William Green recalled:

'We made fires and cooked our meat, took off our belts, sponged out our rifles, got a fresh supply of ammunition, took off our jackets and found plenty of vermin on our bodies, which in some cases had found their way into flesh, as well as appearing outside. As knapsacks and razors and kit were all thrown away, some of the older men had beards like Jews, not having shaved since the commencement of the retreat.'

Next morning, at break of day, Green's patrol was surprised to come across a straggling soldier and his wife, who, by rights, should have reached Corunna the day before:

'We asked the man how it was he was behind his regiment? He belonged to the 91st Scotch. He told us his wife had been taken in labour about 12 o'clock the over night in an out-house or hovel and the doctor of the regiment had attended her. She had been delivered of a fine child. The doctor told the man to stay with his wife and submit to be taken by the enemy. This the soldier agreed to do; but in the morning before daylight appeared, she said to him, "I don't like the thoughts of your going to a French prison and I don't know how ill the French may use me; I will try to get up and walk." She had no shoes or stockings and the babe was wrapped in an apron or shawl. She was almost famished. On the over night we had been served out with three days' bread and pork. We gave her some. She had tasted nothing all the day before. We told them to make the best of their way. Whether the poor woman reached Corunna or died on the road, it is not for me to say. I have often thought of her and talked to others about the affecting scene. They had not left us above half an hour before we had orders not to move until broad daylight appeared, when the advanced guard of the French came in sight at full trot.'

A few rounds from Paget's artillery were enough, however, to dampen the fervour of the French; and the British went so far as to establish a sentry post among the rubble of the ruined bridge:

'Our opponents took up a similar post on their side during the night, so that ... the advanced posts of the contending armies were only the breadth of two arches of a bridge asunder. In this situation we continued for two days, keeping up an incessant fire, so long as we could discover objects to fire at. . . '4

Back in Corunna, the army waited anxiously for the fleet to arrive from Vigo, while Moore set about organising the city's defences. According to William Napier:

'Corunna, although sufficiently strong to compel an enemy to break ground before it, was weakly fortified, and to the southward commanded by heights close to the walls. Moore caused the land front to be strengthened, and occupied the citadel; but he disarmed the sea face of the works, and the inhabitants cheerfully and honourably joined in the labour, although they were aware the army would finally embark, and they would incur the enemy's anger by taking part in the military operations.'

The citizens of Corunna were, perhaps, the first Spaniards whom the British found to be genuinely helpful, sympathetic, and animated by a desire to resist the invader. Schaumann was particularly impressed by the patriotic zeal of the city's governor:

> 'Mounted on an Andalusian stallion, he galloped round the streets, and wherever he found some Spaniards standing idle, he would harangue them, and mingled with kindness and authority urge them to go to the ramparts and help build trenches.'

Even the women pitched in, willingly supplying the batteries with baskets of ammunition, which they carried on their heads.

At first light on 13 January, with the Navy still nowhere in sight, Moore's preparations for departure went on apace. Around mid-morning, these preparations took a dramatic turn when, as William Napier describes, Moore ordered the destruction of 4,000 barrels of gunpowder, hoarded by the Galician *junta*, on a hill three miles beyond the city:

> 'There ensued a crash like the bursting forth of a volcano. The earth trembled for miles, the rocks were torn from their bases, the agitated waters of the harbour rolled the vessels as in a storm, a vast column of smoke and dust, with flames and sparks shooting out from its dark flanks, arose perpendicularly and slowly to a great height, where it burst, and then a shower of stones and fragments of all kinds, descending with a roaring sound, killed many persons who had remained too near the spot.'

The blast had broken virtually every window in Corunna, and for a time terror, panic, and confusion reigned throughout the city:

'The whole town was thrown into considerable alarm,' declared Captain Gordon:

> '...a number of windows were broken by the concussion, and the inhabitants of both sexes rushed into the streets – many of them only half-dressed and with terror in their countenances – and falling on their knees, began to repeat their *Aves* with an energy proportioned to their fright. I was at breakfast at the time this happened, and the idea which first suggested itself to my mind was that the enemy was bombarding the town, and that a shell had fallen upon the house.'

August Schaumann, meanwhile, had been ensconced in a Commissariat office, chatting happily with three hussar quartermasters:

> '...when suddenly two such fierce flashes of lightning and claps of thunder burst over the town that my windows flew into our faces in a thousand pieces, the doors sprang open, the slates rolled from the roof, while I, who had just been rocking myself in my chair and talking, was flung backwards by the gust of hot air that poured in at the window. Even the quartermasters, who believed that a bomb had fallen in the room and burst, ducked under the table. We were almost deaf and the house had been, so to speak, shaken in its foundations. Pulling ourselves together, we stared at each other in dumb amazement, when the streets were suddenly filled with piteous cries. The whole population, particularly the women, who perhaps believed that an earthquake was going to swallow them up, dashed out of their houses with despair written on their faces, and shouting like maniacs, tore the hair from their heads.'

174

Eventually, the true cause of the explosion being revealed, 'stillness, slightly interrupted by the lashing of the waves on the shore, succeeded, and the business of the war went on.'[5]

The artillerymen responsible for the eruption of this mountain of gunpowder risked life and limb in carrying out Moore's instructions, and when the deed was done spent an uncomfortable few minutes as target practice for the French outlying pickets, as Benjamin Miller recorded:

'We had scarcely blown up the magazines before the enemy riflemen came on us and began to fire, but we all made our escape and got safe back to camp, to the great surprise of our army, who thought we were all taken prisoners, and General Moore was heard to say those artillerymen will all be killed or taken prisoners.'

As for Moore, having spent the morning of the 13th making arrangements for the coming battle, he returned to his headquarters on the Canton Grande around 11.00 a. m., utterly exhausted. A couple of hours later, he sat at his desk to pen a final despatch to Castlereagh. Written under obvious strain – betrayed by blotches, smudges, and misspelt words – the letter reveals the disillusionment, contempt, and frustration Sir John now felt for his mission, his Spanish allies, and his army:

'Your Lordship knows that had I followed my own opinion as a military man, I should have retired with the army from Salamanca. The Spanish armies were then beaten; there was no Spanish force to which we could unite; and ... I was satisfied that no efforts would be made to aid us, or favour the cause in which they were engaged. I was sensible, however, that the apathy and indifference of the Spaniards would never have been believed; that, had the British been withdrawn, the loss of the cause would have been imputed to their retreat; and it was necessary to risk this army to convince the people of England, as well as the rest of Europe, that the Spaniards had neither the power, nor the inclination, to make any efforts for themselves. It was for this reason that I marched to

175

Sahagun. As a diversion it succeeded: I brought the whole disposable force of the French against this army, and it has been allowed to follow it, without a single movement being made ... to favour its retreat ... I am sorry to say that the army, whose conduct I had such reason to extol on its march through Portugal, and on its arrival in Spain, has totally changed its character since it began to retreat ... I can say nothing in its favour, but that when there was a prospect of fighting the enemy, the men were then orderly, and seemed pleased, and determined to do their duty ... If I succeed in embarking the army, I shall send it to England – it is quite unfit for further service until it has been refitted, which can best be done there.'

Although the men were probably in better shape than Sir John realised, the horses certainly were not. Schaumann describes how:

'Our artillery and cavalry horses that have reached Corunna and its environs were so weak, worn out, and lame, that some of them dropped dead in the streets, and numbers of others have had to be shot in order to be put out of their misery. Their putrefying bodies, swollen by rain and sun, and bursting in places, are lying under the colonnades in front of the public buildings in the market place, on the quays about the harbour, and in the streets; and while they offend the eye, they fill the air with a pestilential stench of decomposition, that makes one ill. Over 400 of these wretched animals lie about here, and the discharge of pistols, which are adding to their numbers, continues incessantly. Hundreds of horses were killed in the bay outside the town.'

According to Oman:

'The horses were in such a deplorable state that very few of them were worth reshipping: only about 250 cavalry chargers and 700 artillery draught-cattle were considered too good to be left behind. The remainder of the poor beasts, more than 2,000 in number, were shot or stabbed and flung into the sea.'

This was borne out by the 'Soldier of 71st', who claimed that:

'The beach was covered with dead horses, and resounded with the reports of the pistols that were carrying this havoc amongst them. The animals, as if warned by the dead bodies of their fellows, appeared frantic, neighed and screamed in the most frightful manner. Many broke loose and galloped alongst the beach with their manes erect and their mouths wide open.'

Captain Gordon, meanwhile, described the scene in Corunna as:

'. . . exhibiting the appearance of a vast slaughterhouse. Wounded horses, mad with pain, were to be seen running through the streets, and the ground was covered with the mangled carcasses of these noble animals; for, in consequence of their uncertain aim with the pistol, the men were latterly directed to cut the throats of the horses instead of attempting to shoot them.'

The cruel fate of these poor beasts touched the hearts of the troops more profoundly than all the horrors which they had witnessed on the retreat, and cavalrymen broke down and cried for the horses to which, in many cases, they owed their lives. The tragic end of Lord Paget's heroic cavalry chargers is made even more shameful when one considers the verdict of William Napier:

'The very fact of their being so foundered was one of the results of inexperience; the cavalry had come out to Corunna without proper equipments, the horses were ruined, not for want of shoes, but want of hammers and nails to put them on!'

In the early evening of 14 January, finally, 100 naval transports escorted by twelve ships of war hove in sight. They entered the harbour during the night – their progress hindered by so many bloated animal carcasses, bobbing about in the brine – and the embarkation of the cavalry, artillery, and invalids began.

However, some were in no hurry to leave, as Captain Gordon confided to his journal:

> 'I wished to remain on shore until the embarkation of the infantry was effected as I was anxious to be on the spot in case there should be an engagement, although there seemed little probability of such an event. . . '

Notes

1. Moore, James, *Narrative of the Campaign of the British Army in Spain*.
2. Blakeney, Robert, *A Boy in the Peninsular War*.
3. Schaumann's trusty manservant.
4. Blakeney, Robert, *A Boy in the Peninsular War*.
5. Napier, William, *History of the War in the Peninsula*.

A Killing Day

The port of Corunna is situated on a peninsula jutting into the Atlantic, its eastern shore describing a graceful arc, enclosing a capacious haven for shipping. To its southern, landward side, it is enclosed by a series of hills and ridges: the Heights of Santa Margarita and Monte Mero form an inner ring, overlooking both city and anchorage; and a mile or so further south, the Heights of San Cristobal, Peñasquedo, and Palavea, form a higher, more extensive, outer ring. Realising that the chances of quitting Corunna without a fight were virtually nil, Moore had spent much of his time since the 11th surveying this terrain in order to pick the best fighting-ground. Ideally, he would have preferred to make a stand on the outer ring, but he no longer had troops enough to hold such an extensive position. Consequently, he had to make do with the lower ridges of Santa Margarita and Monte Mero. This latter range would constitute Moore's front line and main bastion. At its northern end, the crest commanded Corunna and its harbour; its southern slopes swooped down to the village of Elviña, at the base of the towering Peñasquedo ridge; in the east, it gradually descended to the banks of the broad River Mero; and in the west, it rubbed shoulders with the Heights of San Cristobal and Santa Margarita across a narrow valley, the northern tip of which terminated at the gates of the city. The El-Burgo–Corunna road approached Monte Mero from the south-east, hugging the riverbank, then skirting round the spurs of the Heights of Palavea, before making a diagonal cut across the ridge from the village of Piedralonga on its south-eastern slopes, through Eiris at its centre, and on to Corunna in the north-west.

Since Sir John had lost some 5,000 men on the retreat, and was in the process of shipping his cavalry and artillery – plus 3,000 sick and wounded – he would be left with approximately 15,000 foot soldiers with which to hold this ground. His left flank was fairly secure, being protected by the impassable River Mero, and bolstered by the strong-point of Piedralonga; here he would place Sir John Hope's Division, consisting of Hill's and Leith's Brigades, supported by that of Catlin Crawfurd. His centre and right-centre, however, were directly overlooked by the Heights of Peñasquedo, and would be within range of any French battery posted there, but at least the village of Elviña would provide the sector with a bulwark, against which any advance on the heights might be broken. In this potential killing-ground, he would place Baird's Division, consisting of Manningham's and Bentinck's Brigades, supported by Warde's Foot Guards. As for Sir John's right wing, it was outflanked by the Heights of San Cristobal, the Monte de Mesoiro, and the western tip of the Heights of Peñasquedo, and was liable to be turned by any advance from these hills. Moore was aware of this weakness, and decided to invite Soult to exploit it, by leaving his right wing 'refused', that is to say, denuded of troops. But Moore's Achilles' heel would hide a powerful kick, for he intended to hold back his remaining forces – consisting of the 6,000 troops of Fraser's and Paget's Divisions – in and around Corunna, ready to make a counter-punch when needed. Of the nine light guns (6-pounders) which Sir John planned to keep ashore, six were to be ranged in pairs along the ridge, and the remaining three allotted to General Paget. Moore decided to direct any serious fighting in person, seconded by his fellow-Scots, Baird and Hope.

Despite Sir John's tireless preparations for battle – not to mention the reviving spirits of his troops – some senior officers

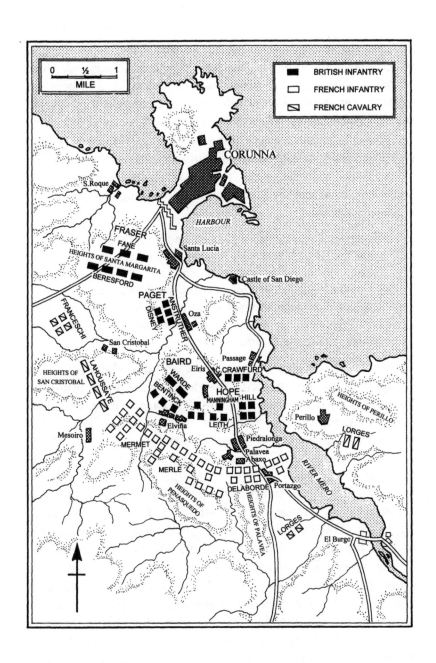

thought the situation so perilous, so desperate, as to warrant peace talks with Soult. But Sir John rejected the suggestion out of hand. Although his army had dwindled in numbers, its fighting capability had been boosted considerably by its sojourn in Corunna, where the soldiers had received rest, food – and perhaps more importantly – brand new muskets plus a plentiful supply of ammunition. Consequently, there would be no parleying with the enemy and no surrender. Besides which, according to August Schaumann, the prevailing mood was one of cheery defiance:

> 'Everybody, young and old, rich and poor, alike – aye, even the women and girls – [was] busy on the ramparts helping to throw up entrenchments...
>
> When I was not on duty I spent my time in the cafés and confectioners' shops. I spent my evenings laughing and joking in the company of ladies, and often had drinking bouts with other officers.'

Meanwhile, Soult's advance on Corunna – brought to an abrupt halt on the 11th with the destruction of the bridge at El-Burgo and the aggressive stance of Paget's Reserve – had resumed again on the 13th. For on that day, Franceschi's scouts had discovered an alternative passage over the Mero, seven miles inland at Celas, and within hours, his hussars and dragoons had begun pouring onto the hostile bank. Paget, isolated at El-Burgo, stood in danger of encirclement and was withdrawn by Moore to the safety of Corunna the same afternoon. This evacuation was a gift to Soult, who promptly had the El-Burgo bridge repaired and marched his men across in the night. The marshal's progress, however, had been prudent, protracted, precise. This was due, in part, to a healthy respect for Moore's rearguard, though the primary cause of his caution lay in the fact that his army was understrength, being weakened by straggling, the loss of Heudelet's Division – still floundering hopelessly in the rear – and the absence of Delaborde's, which, having fallen behind on the march, was struggling to catch up. When this unit finally made its appearance on the 15th, Soult's force numbered some 15,500 infantry, 4,500 cavalry, and thirty-six guns. Confident at last of his strength, the Duke of Damnation resumed the hunt for Moore in earnest, gaining the Heights of Palavea and Peñasquedo later that day. He was greeted upon arrival by bullets from the British pickets, while Moore, believing a battle to be imminent, sallied forth from Corunna and into position on Monte Mero. An abortive bayonet-charge against the French guns, led by Colonel MacKenzie of the 5th Regiment – who got himself killed in the process – brought the day's action to a close and, as evening fell, hostilities dwindled to an uneasy truce: 'Thus were the two armies in sight of one another,' wrote Charles Stewart, 'without any serious disposition being exhibited to bring matters to the issue of a battle. . . '

The morning of 16 January dawned misty and cold. At 6.00 a.m. Sir John Moore, mounting a cream and black charger, made a tour of his outposts on Monte Mero, the better to gauge the intentions of his enemy. As his soldiers quietly cooked breakfast, cleaned their equipment, or picked the lice from their bodies, the Commander of the Forces gazed across the valley to the heights opposite. There, too, the scene appeared tranquil. When would Soult attack? Surely he would not let the army embark unmolested and slip from his grasp into the embrace of the sea? Moore snapped his telescope shut, tugged at his horse's reins and, eager to continue shipping his baggage and stores, cantered back to the harbour at Corunna.

Around noon, according to James Moore, Sir John sent for Colonel Anderson, his adjutant-general,[1] in order to finalise arrangements for the embarkation of the troops:

> '[Sir John] directed that he [Anderson] must continue to send sick men, horses, and baggage aboard the ships as quickly as possible, but that he wished all the boats to be disengaged at four in the afternoon; for he intended, if the French did not move, to begin embarking the Reserve at that hour. And that he would go out himself, as soon as it was dark, to send in the troops by brigades in the order he wished them

to embark. He continued transacting business until a little after one o'clock, when his horse was brought. He then took leave of Colonel Anderson, saying, "Remember, I depend upon your paying particular attention to everything that concerns the embarkation; and let there be as little confusion as possible."'

Meanwhile, the morning mists having cleared, Marshal Soult was presented with a fine view of the British position on Monte Mero. From his elevated platform on the Heights of Peñasquedo, he was pleased to note that his adversary's line lay within range of his guns, and that it was outflanked in the west by his left wing (Moore's right). Consequently, he adopted the plan anticipated by Sir John: first he would bombard the British front line, in order to soften it up; then, while containing its left and centre with the divisions of Delaborde and Merle – some 11,000 troops in total – he would send the 6,000 infantrymen of Mermet's Division, supported by Lahoussaye's 1,500 horsemen, to hit its exposed right flank, turn it, and roll up the remaining regiments from west to east. Thus the marshal envisaged the annihilation of Moore's army – or its encirclement and capture at the very least – and was simply waiting for his army to complete a difficult deployment over rough, rocky, uneven ground, before firing the first shot.

Across the valley, however, Moore was feverishly checking his watch, and by 1.30 p. m. had virtually abandoned the idea of a battle. It was around this time that he began moving the regiments of the Reserve down to the harbour ready for embarkation; and even Captain Gordon of the 15th Hussars – who had lingered on shore in the hope of seeing a battle – was finally:

'. . .obliged reluctantly to bid *adieu* to Corunna . . . and to proceed to my floating dungeon, where I was speedily driven below by violent attacks of sea-sickness.'

Meanwhile, on the ridge above Elviña, Captain James MacCarthy of the 50th Regiment was somewhat surprised to see a woman, with a newborn babe in her arms, make her way across no-man's-land to the British lines:

> 'She was an Irish woman, the wife of a soldier of the
> Light Company of the 50th Regiment, had lain-in on
> the march, was kindly attended by doctors of the
> French army, supported at the expense of Marshal
> Soult, arrived with his baggage, and was . . . sent over
> with Soult's compliments, that he should soon visit the
> 50th Regiment . . . The ensigns of the 50th Regiment
> – Moore and Stewart – unfurled the colours by order
> of Major Napier;[2] who, in allusion to Marshal Soult's
> message, bravely said, "Open the colours that they
> may see the 50th!"'

A deserter confirmed the marshal's intention to attack, and
when, at around 2.00 p.m., *voltigeurs* were seen advancing
beyond the French picket line, the redcoats 'began to think it
a signal for a general action or a "killing day" as soldiers term
it.'[3] Thus, according to Major Napier's youngest brother
William:

> '. . .20,000 French veterans opened this battle against
> 14,000 British, who, having but nine six-pounders to
> oppose to a numerous light artillery, were also galled
> by eleven heavy guns on the rocks: and soon that
> formidable battery opened the fight with a slaughtering
> fire, sending its bullets crashing through the English
> ranks from right to centre.'

Moore's spirit was awakened by the sound of the guns. At
last, after labouring for so long under the dark clouds of
disappointment and despair, the storm was about to burst,
bestowing upon him a final chance to silence his critics. . .

Meanwhile, the French shot fell thick and fast among his
troops on the ridge, interrupting the culinary efforts of
artilleryman Benjamin Miller, who was in the middle of
cooking potatoes:

> '. . . the shot came and knocked the kettle off the fire.
> We filled our pockets with them half-boiled and ate
> them while fighting our guns.'

For the 'Private of the 42nd' the opening of the cannonade
was a baptism of fire:

'I had thought nothing of battle till now; we were within reach of the enemy's shot. There was a kind of fear on me which I think every man is struck with at first; I was never in a great battle before.'

And as for Robert Blakeney and the men of the 28th Regiment, they were blithely *en route* for the transports, dreaming of home, when the bedlam began:

'We had not proceeded above a hundred yards when we heard the firing of guns. The division halted to a man, as if by word of command; each looked with anxious enquiry. But we were not long kept in suspense. An *aide-de-camp* came galloping at full speed to arrest our progress, telling us that an extraordinary movement was taking place throughout the enemy's line; the three guns fired were a signal to give notice. We instantly counter-marched, and passed through the village of Los Ayres [Eiris?], where but twenty minutes before we had bidden *adieu* to Spain, and considered ourselves on the way to England.'

As the guns boomed from the battery on the Heights of Peñasquedo, wreaking havoc among Baird's men above Elviña, Mermet's Division, consisting of two infantry regiments – the 31st and 47th of the Line – led by 600 *voltigeurs*, advanced towards the western tip of Monte Mero with cries of *'En avant, tue, tue, en avant tue!'* According to the 'Private of the 42nd':

'The French army did not advance very rapidly, on account of the badness of the ground. Our colonel gave orders for us to lie on the ground, at the back of the height our position was on; and whenever the French were within a few yards of us, we were to start up and fire our muskets, and then give them the bayonet.'

Meanwhile, on Moore's far right, the eight regiments of Lahoussaye's and Franceschi's cavalry crept down the slopes of Monte de Mesoiro, threatening to bypass the British front and make a beeline up the valley to Corunna.

They were to be supported in this manoeuvre by the 47th of the Line, which had begun arcing its way round Moore's right flank; while the 31st crashed straight into Elviña, drove out the British pickets, and continued up the slopes of Monte Mero. Above them, waiting on the crest, were the bayonets of Bentinck's Brigade, consisting of the 4th, 42nd, and 50th Regiments. Major Charles Napier, in command of the 50th, was set to intervene, when Moore arrived to take charge:

> 'I asked him to let me throw our grenadiers, who were losing men fast, into the enclosures in front. "No," he said, "they will fire on our own pickets in the village." "Sir, our pickets and those of the 4th Regiment also, were driven from thence when you went to the left." "Were they? Then you are right, send out your grenadiers," and again he galloped away. Turning round I saw Captain Clunes of the 50th, just arrived from Corunna, and said to him, "Clunes, take your grenadiers and open the ball." He stalked forward alone, like Goliath before the Philistines, for six feet five he was in height, and of proportionate bulk and strength: his grenadiers followed and thus the battle began on our side.'[4]

And there it was to stay. For while Moore's left and centre remained relatively undisturbed till late afternoon, his right was constantly engaged, soaking up the punishment from Soult's incessant bombardment and successive attacks. Bentinck's Brigade bore the brunt of this onslaught, and as the troops continued to take a pounding from the French guns, Moore returned to share the danger and steady their nerves, as Charles Napier reported:

> 'A shot had torn off the leg of a 42nd man, who screamed horribly, and rolled about so as to excite agitation and alarm with others. The General said, "This is nothing my lads, keep your ranks; take that man away: my good fellow don't make such a noise, we must bear these things better." He spoke sharply but it had a good effect; for this man's cries had made an opening in the ranks, and the men shrunk from the

spot, although they had not done so when others had been hit who did not cry out.'

No less a victim of this galling fire was Sir David Baird himself, his left arm smashed by a roundshot. With Baird taken to the rear, Moore remained in the thick of the action, directing events from the front line. One British veteran observed that:

> 'The roar of cannon and the roll of musketry was so loud that without attention the word of command could scarcely be given, and the sound of the bugle hardly heard.'[5]

Noticing the turning movement of the 47th of the Line on his right, and the cavalry picking its way forward (fortunately with obvious difficulty over the broken ground), Sir John galloped over to his exposed flank, where Colonel Wynch's 4th Regiment was holding the line. He ordered Wynch to swing back from the firing line at a right angle – rather like a door on a hinge – in order to face off the coming threat: 'The manoeuvre was carried out with such precision,' commented Sir Charles Oman:

> '. . . as to win his outspoken approval, "That is exactly how it should be done," he shouted to Colonel Wynch, and then rode off to attend to the 50th and 42nd, further to his left.'

Meanwhile, Major-General Bentinck (second son of William Henry Cavendish Bentinck, the Prime Minister and 3rd Duke of Portland) had taken an interest in events and decided to join Charles Napier in the firing line for a chat:

> 'Lord William Bentinck now came up on his quiet mule, and though the fire was heavy, began talking to me as if we were going to breakfast; his manner was his ordinary one, with perhaps an increase of good-humour and placidity. He conversed for some time, but no recollection of what he said remains, for the fire was sharp and my eyes were more busy than my ears:

I only remember saying to myself, "This chap takes it coolly, or the devil's in it!"'

Moments later, Moore returned in time to witness the French column, toiling up the slopes towards him, split in two and deploy prior to a final rush on the summit of the ridge. Seizing the moment, Moore ordered Colonel Sterling of the 42nd Highlanders to counter-attack, and the troops – who had been lying down – leaped up, cheered, let loose a volley, and charged, as the 'Private of the 42nd' recalled:

> 'All the word of command that was given was, "Forty-Second, charge!" In one moment every man was up with a cheer, and the sound of his musket, and every shot did execution. They were so close upon us that we gave them the bayonet the instant we fired ... We followed them down to the valley, and stopped not for general or commanding officer; but still on, in the rage and wrath of the Highlanders ... As we pursued them down the hill there was a poor Frenchman sorely wounded, and on his knees, his hands uplifted, and pleading for quarter. My next man, a robust Highlander, in his rage, exclaimed, "You Buonaparte man! She'll run her through!" [*sic*] With a sudden jerk of my musket I threw his on his shoulder, and the poor fellow's life was saved.'

Thus two of Bentinck's three regiments were now embroiled in a battle royal: Colonel Wynch's 4th Regiment pouring shot into the French troops on the extreme right; while Colonel Sterling's Highlanders were chasing *voltigeurs* down Monte Mero. Only Charles Napier's 50th remained without orders. His men were, however, still serving as a mark for the French gunners on the opposite heights and Napier ordered the regimental colours – unfurled so defiantly a few hours before – to be lowered:

> 'I walked up and down before the regiment, and made the men shoulder and order arms twice, to occupy their attention, for they were falling fast and seemed uneasy at standing under fire.'

At 3.00 p. m. Napier still had no orders and, with mounting frustration, he turned to John Montgomery – an old soldier who had risen through the ranks – for support:

> '"Good God Montgomery!" I said, "are we not to advance?" "I think we ought," he answered. "But," said I, "no orders have come." "I would not wait," he said. The 4th did not move, the 42nd seemed likely to want our aid, it was not a moment for hesitation, and John Montgomery, a Scotchman, said laughingly, "You cannot be wrong to follow the 42nd." I gave the word but forbad any firing, and to prevent it, and occupy the men's attention, made them slope and carry arms by word of command. Many of them cried out, "Major let us fire!" "Not yet," was my answer, for having advanced without orders, I thought to have them more under command if we were wrong, whereas if firing once begun we could not change.'

Napier's men gladly marched into the maelstrom, anything being better than passively waiting to be blown up by a French shell. John Wilson was particularly pleased to join the action, having taken the trouble to don his finest uniform – painstakingly preserved during the rigours of the retreat – for the moment he would finally 'meet Master Soult.'[6]

Napier caught up with the 42nd at the entrance to Elviña, his troops by now desperate to open fire:

> 'I said to my men, "Do you see your enemies plain enough to hit them?" "By Jasus we do!" "Then blaze away!" And such a rolling fire broke out as I have hardly heard since.'

Moore, looking on from the heights, was delighted and called out, 'Well done 50th! Well done my majors!'[7] as Napier disappeared from view.

Leaving the 42nd behind, Napier led his men into Elviña and was immediately brought up short by a breast-high wall. Major Charles Banks Stanhope, Napier's deputy, promptly clambered over, calling on the men to follow, but only a few of the bravest obeyed, so Napier grabbed a sergeant's pike

and, damning and cursing, prodded the rest over. He then led
his force further into the village, amid a hail of bullets fired
from the houses:

> 'Still I led the men on, followed closely by Ensigns
> Moore and Stewart with the colours, until both fell and
> the colours were caught up by Sergeant Magee and
> another sergeant. My sword-belt was shot off, scabbard
> and all, but not being hit, I pushed rapidly into the
> street . . . Many Frenchmen lay there, apparently dead,
> and the soldiers cried out, "Bayonet them, they are
> pretending!" The idea was to me terrible, and made
> me call out, "No! No! Leave those cowards, there are
> plenty who bear arms to kill, come on!"'

Nearby stood a church, and beyond it a rocky mound,
behind which the survivors of William Clunes' Grenadier
Company were pinned down by French fire, coming from the
far end of a long narrow lane. Napier joined the grenadiers,
and tried to rouse his combined force to the attack, but with
only a handful of officers left to second him, he could not get
the men to budge. Electing to lead by example, Napier broke
cover and charged up the lane solo, calling for the rest to
follow. He was joined by three officers and thirty devoted
privates:

> 'The fire was then terrible, many shells burst among us,
> and the crack of these things deafened me, making my
> ears ring. Half way up the lane I fell, without knowing
> why, yet was much hurt, though at the moment
> unconscious of it; a soldier cried out, "The Major is
> killed!" "Not yet, come on!" . . . We reached the end
> of this murderous lane, but a dozen of those who
> entered it with me fell ere we got through it.'

Napier's survivors emerged from the lane and took shelter
behind a breastwork of loose stones, thrown up the previous
day by the pickets of the 4th Regiment. The intrepid Major
saw that by another dash, his party would be upon a battery
of French guns, and the thought of gaining such a prize filled
his mind with reckless notions of glory. At any rate, it was

impossible to stay put for, having advanced so far, Napier's party was vulnerable to hostile fire from the front, and 'friendly' fire from the rear. Within seconds, four of Napier's companions were hit – two dropped by French bullets, and two by British:

> 'The poor fellows kept crying out as they died, "Oh God! Major, our own men are killing us! Oh Christ God, I'm shot in the back of the head!" The last man was so, for he fell against me, and the ball had entered just above the poll.[8] Remembering then that my father had saved a man's life at the Siege of Charleston, by pulling a ball out with his finger before inflammation swelled the parts, I thought to do the same, but could not find it, and feared to do harm by putting my finger far in. It made me feel sick, and the poor fellow, being laid down, continued crying out that our men had killed him, and there he soon died.'

By his own admission, Napier was now in shock, and began stamping his feet in rage and despair, believing that his troops had abandoned him:

> 'I sent Turner, Harrison and Patterson, the three officers with me, to bring them on, and they found Stanhope animating the men, but not knowing what to do, and calling out, "Good God! where is Napier?" When Turner told him I was in front and raging for them to come on for an attack on the battery, he [Stanhope] gave a shout and called on the men to follow him, but ere taking a dozen strides, cried out, "Oh my God!" and fell dead, shot through the heart.'[9]

Lieutenant Turner, accompanied by a sergeant, dashed back up the lane to inform Napier that the men could not be moved, whereupon the frantic major jumped on the wall and, waving his hat and sword, yelled at the troops to come on: 'My own companions called out to jump down or I should be killed: I thought so too, but was so mad as to care little what happened to me.' Little did he know that one chivalrous French officer had prevented his men from firing at him; or that another, overcome with admiration for his bravery, had been restrained from rushing forward to embrace him!

Eventually giving up on the 50th, Napier dropped down from the wall and, telling his companions to remain where they were, went off in search of the 42nd, still dreaming of an assault on the French guns. He was, however, hopelessly lost and, after wandering about for a time, returned to find that his comrades – less than happy at being caught between two fires – had forsaken him:

'I felt very miserable then, thinking the 50th had behaved ill; that my not getting the battery had been a cause of the battle being lost, and that Moore would attribute all to me ... The battle seemed nearly over, I thought myself the last man alive belonging to our side who had got so far in front, and felt certain of death ... In this state of distraction, and still under a heavy fire, I turned down the lane to rejoin the regiment and soon came on a wounded man, who shrieked out, "Oh praise be to God Major! My dear Major! God help you my darling, one of your own 50th." "I cannot carry you," was my reply, "can you walk with my help?" "Oh no, Major, I am too badly wounded." "You must lie there, then, till help can be found." "Oh Christ God, my jewel, my own dear Major, sure you won't leave me!" The agony with which he screamed was great, it roused all my feelings, and strange to say, alarmed me about my own danger, which had been forgot in my misery at finding Harrison was gone ... and thinking the battle lost. Stooping down, I raised the poor fellow, but a musket-ball just then broke the small bone of my leg some inches above the ankle. . . '

Chapter 11

Notes

1. Lieutenant-Colonel Paul Anderson, Moore's friend and comrade of over twenty years, had taken over the role of adjutant-general since Brigadier-General Clinton's confinement to bed with dysentery.
2. Charles James Napier (1782–1853) was the eldest of the three Napier brothers on the campaign.
3. Miller, Benjamin, *Adventures of Serjeant Benjamin Miller.*
4. Captain William Clunes was later wounded in the fight for Elviña but survived the battle. Charles Napier's account can be found in the biography written by his brother James, *The Life and Opinions of General Sir Charles Napier.*
5. Green, William, *Where Duty Calls Me.*
6. According to MacCarthy, Lieutenant John Wilson was killed in the bitter battle for Elviña.
7. Napier and Stanhope were both devoted to Moore and considered his *protégés.*
8. Above the hairline.
9. Stanhope's obituary appeared in *The Gentleman's Magazine* of March 1809: 'The fatal bullet had passed through the heart of the deceased; and so instantaneous must have been the death of Major Stanhope, that a sense of pain had not torn from his countenance that smile which the bravery of his soldiers and the applause of his commander excited.'

CHAPTER 12

I Hope My Country
Will Do Me Justice

Napier's attack upon Elviña – though successful at first – had left his regiment badly disorganised, and when the French began to feed in reserves the position of the 50th became increasingly precarious. Napier – stranded far in advance of his soldiers – may have believed himself deserted, but the fact was that the 50th were suffering heavily from intensifying French fire. To make matters worse, the men had used up their ammunition during the initial fire-fight – Captain James MacCarthy being reduced to taking the buttons off his jacket and firing them from a discarded cavalry carbine – and as a consequence had been obliged to take cover behind the village church. Here, according to MacCarthy (soon to receive a bullet in the left thigh):

> '... they became a barrier, sustaining the enemy's fire; and making arrangements for maintaining their position with the bayonet, kept the enemy at bay without being possessed of a single cartridge.'

Observing events from his ridge, Moore ordered Bentinck to send reinforcements to the aid of the 50th, but the brigadier saw fit to disobey and, shortly after the death of Stanhope, went so far as to recall the regiment to the relative safety of the heights. Thus Napier, who was generally believed to have been killed, was finally abandoned for good and Mermet retook Elviña.

Soon French troops began pouring out of the village and on towards Monte Mero for another attempt on Moore's line. Their path was blocked by the men of the 42nd, who like the 50th were out of ammunition, but unlike the 50th had not been pulled out of danger. Thus, as Mermet's men came on, the soldiers of the 42nd fretfully looked round for support. Aware of their predicament, and of the pressing need to stall the French advance, Sir John threw forward the two battalions of Warde's 1st Foot Guards, but as soon as the hard-pressed Highlanders saw fresh troops heading their way, they assumed they were being relieved and, quitting their position, headed back up the slopes. Moore contained this crisis by plunging into the ranks of the retreating Highlanders, standing in his stirrups, and yelling, 'My brave 42nd ... you still have your bayonets! Think on Scotland!' This appeal to cold courage and national honour was enough, and the Scottish troops – Moore's own countrymen – promptly turned about and marched back into the brawl. Sir John, smiling in appreciation, doffed his hat as they went. Two seconds later, he dropped from his horse, hit, like Baird, by a French roundshot.

He fell at the feet of Colonel Thomas Graham's horse and, as he had made no cry, Graham at first thought that all was well. He was soon undeceived, however, for Moore had received an appalling injury, as described by his *aide-de-camp*, Henry Hardinge:

> 'I had been ordered by the Commander-in-Chief to desire a battalion of the Guards to advance ... and I was pointing out to the General the situation of the battalion, and our horses were touching, at the very moment that a cannon-shot from the enemy's battery carried away his left shoulder and part of the collar-bone, leaving the arm hanging by the flesh. The violence of the stroke threw him off his horse, on his back. Not a muscle of his face altered, nor did a sigh betray the least sensation of pain ... The blood flowed

fast; but the attempt to stop it with my sash was useless, from the size of the wound. Sir John assented to being removed in a blanket to the rear. In raising him for that purpose, his sword, hanging on the wounded side, touched his arm, and became entangled between his legs. I perceived the inconvenience, and was in the act of unbuckling it from his waist, when he said, "It is as well as it is. I had rather it should go out of the field with me."'

Suffering unspeakable pain, Moore still strained to see the advance of the 42nd, all the time squeezing Hardinge's hand. In fact, the general seemed so composed that the aide suggested that he might recover: 'No, Hardinge,' replied Sir John, 'I feel that to be impossible.' Moore was borne off the field by six men of the 42nd led by a sergeant: 'You need not go with me,' he told Hardinge, 'Report to General Hope that I am wounded and carried to the rear.' And so, leaving the sergeant to his charge, Hardinge galloped off to inform a stunned Sir John Hope that – Moore and Baird both having been wounded – the command had devolved upon him.

The six Scotsmen carried Moore along the Santa Lucia road to Corunna, stopping several times to turn about, in order that he might see or hear the battle raging in the rear. Presently, two surgeons appeared, sent by Baird, who, having had his wounded arm dressed (it would be amputated at the shoulder on the voyage back to Plymouth), had told them to 'stop fussing' and find Sir John. Moore, however, also dismissed them, saying, 'You can be of no service to me. Go to the soldiers to whom you may be useful.' Nevertheless, Surgeon McGill of the 1st Foot (Royal Scots), examined the wound, carefully removing some cloth and two buttons before pronouncing it 'a hopeless case'. Moments later, the wounded Colonel Wynch arrived on the scene in a cart, and it was suggested that the Highlanders give up their burden; they bluntly refused, claiming that they could provide Sir John with a smoother ride. Moore smiled faintly and whispered, 'I think so too.' Thus the sad procession continued on its way, arriving at Corunna under the gaze of a gaggle of shocked onlookers, including August Schaumann:

> 'Among many wounded men who were borne past us into the town there appeared at about 4 o'clock a party of several *aides-de-camp* and officers, marching very slowly and sadly behind six soldiers bearing a wounded man in a blood-stained blanket slung upon two poles. Two doctors walked on either side of the litter, and repeatedly cast anxious looks inside it. It was General Moore.'

Sir John's bearers arrived before his quarters with silent tears streaming down dirty faces. They were met by the General's servant, François, struck dumb by the awful spectacle: 'My friend, this is nothing,' Moore sighed. He was then placed on a mattress, on the floor of a darkened room, and Colonel Paul Anderson – his friend for over twenty years – remained with him, holding his hand, while straining to catch his words:

> 'He seemed very anxious to speak to me, and at intervals, got out as follows: "Anderson, you know that I have always wished to die this way." He then asked, "Are the French beaten?" Which he repeated to everyone he knew, as they came in. "I hope the people of England will be satisfied . . . I hope my country will do me justice . . . Anderson, you will see my friends as soon as you can . . . tell them . . . everything. Say to my mother. . . " Here his voice quite failed and he was excessively agitated: "Hope, Hope, I have much to say to him . . . but I cannot get it out . . . Are Colonels Graham and all my *aides-de-camp* well?"[1] He then asked Major Colborne if the French were beaten? And on being told they were on every point, he said, "It's a great satisfaction for me to know we have beaten the French . . . I fear I shall be long in dying. It is great uneasiness . . . it is great pain." He thanked the surgeons for their trouble. Captains Percy and Stanhope, two of his *aides-de-camp*, then came into the room. He spoke kindly to them both and asked Percy

if all his *aides-de-camp* were well? After some interval he said, "Stanhope, remember me to your sister."[2] He pressed my hand close to his body, and in a few minutes died without a struggle.'

Moore's life ended at 8.00 p. m. but the Battle of Corunna faded before him, a winter's night closing the combat, with both sides occupying roughly the same ground they had done in the morning. The left of the British line had not been seriously assailed until around 4.30 p. m., when Delaborde's troops advanced into Piedralonga, evicting the British pickets. Fierce fighting ensued, much of it hand-to-hand, as the rival armies grappled for possession of the village, but when the bloodshed ceased about 6.00 p. m., neither side had gained any significant territorial advantage. Meanwhile, on the British right, Mermet's outflanking manoeuvre had been checked by the 4th Regiment, then stopped in its tracks by the timely arrival of Paget's Division. The French offensive had been severely hampered by broken terrain, criss-crossed by walls and gulleys, and the troops – especially the cavalry – had found it difficult to deploy. They were eventually shunted back by the sharpshooters of the 52nd and 95th Regiments. Around Elviña, Mermet, aided by Merle, had continued to throw troops into the attack, but although he managed to maintain a presence in the village – its streets choked with dead and dying – he found it impossible to break out, due to an advance by Manningham's Brigade, supported later by that of Leith.

In short, the British had fought Soult to a standstill, repulsing his attacks at every point; and though they were not in a position to exploit their success with an offensive, the redcoats had secured their embarkation, and thus claimed the Battle of Corunna (known as the Battle of Elviña to the Spaniards) as a victory. This was a view apparently shared – at least initially – by the Duke of Damnation himself, who announced that he could not prolong the fight without the aid of reinforcements. Losses in the battle were never accurately assessed – Hope's figure of some 700–800 British dead and wounded is certainly an overestimate – but it is generally accepted that the British inflicted twice as many casualties as they sustained.

Shortly after 8.00 p.m. the band of mourners around Moore's body broke up and, mindful of their duties, disappeared into the bitter night. Captain James Stanhope stalked back to the battlefield in a fit of despair. Happening upon George Napier, his friend and fellow *aide-de-camp*, it was agreed that they should go in search of their brothers. Stanhope found the body of his brother Charles easily enough, as it had been borne off the field and brought back to the British lines. As for Charles Napier, there was still no sign.

Yet Charles Napier was still alive – if not exactly well – and a mere two miles distant, at the headquarters of General Hilaire-Benoît Reynaud, one of Merle's brigade commanders. He had survived the battle for Elviña against all odds, but he owed his life to the most unlikely of guardian angels – a French drummer boy by the name of Guibert...

When Napier had recovered, somewhat, from the shock of being shot in the leg, he hobbled off in search of his comrades with the piteous cries of the wounded soldier still ringing in his ears. He eventually made it back to the village church, but the 50th had pulled out long before, and the only redcoats to be seen were four stranded soldiers who, like himself, had been cut off from their regiments and left behind. Napier joined this forlorn group, as they huddled at the entrance to the church, their backs to the door. Moments later, French troops were spotted advancing towards them via two lanes which ran up to the church. Napier thought to make a stand, and immediately leaped forward with a shout; but at that precise moment, the door of the church opened in their rear, and in an instant, French bayonets were upon them:

> 'I felt a stab in the back: it gave me no pain, but felt cold and threw me on my face. Turning to rise, I saw the man who had stabbed me making a second thrust; whereupon, letting go my sabre, I caught his bayonet by the socket, turned the thrust, and raising myself by the exertion, grasped his firelock with both hands, thus in mortal struggle regaining my feet.'

His companions were killed in an instant, but Napier continued to struggle with his assailant:

> 'That was a contest for life, and being the strongest, I forced him between myself and his comrades, who appeared to be the men whose lives I had saved when they pretended to be dead on our advance through the village. They struck me with their muskets clubbed, and bruised me much; whereupon, seeing no help, and being overpowered by numbers, and in great pain from my wounded leg, I called out, "*Je me rends*,"[3] remembering the expression correctly from an old story of a fat officer, whose name being James, called out "Jemmy round!"'

Engulfed by Frenchmen, the major continued, nevertheless, to fight for his life, all the time growing fainter. Moments later, however, a swarthy man appeared, brandishing a brass-hilted sabre, and struck Napier a blow across the head which cut into the bone:

> 'Fire sparkled from my eyes, I fell on my knees, blinded, yet without quite losing my senses, and holding still on to the musket. Recovering in a moment, I regained my legs and saw a florid handsome young French drummer holding the arm of the dark Italian, who was in the act of repeating the blow. Quarter was then given, but they tore my pantaloons in tearing my watch and purse from my pocket, and a little locket of hair which hung round my neck; they snatched at everything: but while this went on two of them were wounded, and the drummer, Guibert, ordered the dark man who had sabred me to take me to the rear.'

As soon as Guibert's back was turned, however, the Italian drew his sword once more, bent on finishing Napier off:

> 'I called out to the drummer, "This rascal is going to kill me! Brave Frenchmen don't kill prisoners!" Guibert ran back, swore furiously at the Italian, shoved him away, almost down, and putting his arms round my waist, supported me himself: thus this generous

Frenchman saved me twice, for the Italian was bent upon slaying.'

Napier limped up the lane with Guibert's help, when they suddenly came face to face with a solitary soldier of the 50th, striding swiftly towards them. The soldier stopped – bent on standing his ground – raised his musket, and stared intently at the party:

> 'I threw up his musket, calling out, "For God's sake don't fire, I am a prisoner, badly wounded, and can't help you – surrender!" "For why should I surrender?" He called aloud with the deepest of all Irish brogues, "Because there at least twenty men upon you!" (There were five or six with us at the time.) "Well if I must surrender, there!" said he, dashing down his firelock across their legs and making them jump, "There's my firelock for yez." Then coming up close he threw his arm round me, and giving Guibert a push that sent him and one or two more reeling against the wall, shouted out, "Stand away, ye bloody spalpeens, I'll carry him myself, bad luck to the whole of yez!"'

The Irishman's name was John Hennessy and, happily, Guibert and his companions thought better of tackling him; instead, he was permitted to take hold of Napier and like a pair of drunkards, they stumbled off down the lane to captivity.[4]

Later that night, across the valley at Corunna, August Schaumann opened his journal and put pen to paper:

> 'Everybody is particularly distressed about General Moore. I returned home almost wild with sorrow at what I had seen and heard. At ten o'clock in the evening, the victorious English troops gradually marched into the town in the finest order to embark. They were all in tatters, hollow-eyed, and covered with blood and filth. They looked so terrible that the people of Corunna made the sign of the cross as they passed.'

According to Sir John Hope:

'The troops quitted their position about ten at night, with a degree of order that did them credit. The whole of the artillery that remained unembarked, having been withdrawn, the troops followed in the order prescribed, and marched to their respective points of embarkation in the town and neighbourhood of Corunna.'

Eager to be away on the following day's tide, Hope immediately began forwarding men to the water's edge, where the Jack tars of the Royal Navy were waiting to receive them, as John Dobbs of the 52nd recalled:

'...we found the boats waiting for us and immediately pushed off, but lost one another in the darkness, and some of us not knowing where to find our ships got on board the first we came to, sending back the boats for others who were waiting for them.'

Meanwhile, on the field of battle, the pickets remained at their posts, tending huge fires to deceive the French, while the brigades of Beresford and Hill remained in Corunna to cover the embarkation.

At midnight, Moore's remains were carried to Colonel Graham's quarters in the Citadel, prior to interment. The general had always maintained that, should he die in battle, he wished to be buried where he fell; consequently, it was decided to bury him on the landward side of the citadel's ramparts. The service – a hasty affair – was conducted by Reverend Henry Symons of the Guards early next day. James Moore recorded the scene:

'A grave was dug by a party of the 9th Regiment, the *aides-de-camp* attending by turns. No coffin could be procured, and the body was never undressed, but wrapped up by the officers of his staff in a military cloak and blankets ...Towards eight o'clock in the morning some firing was heard. It was then resolved to finish the interment, lest a serious attack should be made; on which the officers would be ordered away, and not suffered to pay the last duties to their general ...The officers of his family bore the body to the grave; the funeral service was read by the chaplain, and the corpse was covered with earth.'

The firing heard by the mourners at Moore's graveside had been occasioned by a cautious French advance, for Soult, having discovered the British withdrawal, had begun closing in on Corunna, and by noon had pushed a battery of six guns onto the heights above the southern tip of the bay. Captain Gordon, by now aboard the *Martha* transport, saw the French guns arrive:

> 'The French did not show themselves until the morning was pretty well advanced when, finding that all our posts were called in, they pushed forward some troops and artillery to the heights above St Lucia, and opened a cannonade upon the shipping in the harbour, which caused great confusion amongst the transports. Many were obliged to cut their cables, some suffered damage by running foul of each other, and five or six were abandoned by their crews and drifted on shore. The whole of this disorder was occasioned by the masters of the vessels, who paid no attention to the signals to "weigh anchor and stand into the bay," which had been made repeatedly since break of day.'

In fact, four transports ran aground, three of which had to be burned, their cargo of men ferried to other vessels in the harbour in a confused operation, during which nine men of the Royal Waggon Train were drowned.

Meanwhile, according to the 'Soldier of the 71st', 'The ships-of-war soon silenced the French guns and we saw no more of them.'

Thus, in an atmosphere of mounting tension and anxiety, the embarkation continued apace. William Green of the 95th was one of those who was evacuated:

> 'We marched through the streets into the harbour ... the boats of the men-of-war and transport ships pushed to the shore to take us on board; but what confusion was there! Many of the hussars' horses were galloping on the beach like mad things. There was not

time to embark them. Several were shot or we should have been rode over or trodden to death.'

Back at the Citadel, however, August Schaumann was still packing and preparing to quit his billet:

> 'The lady of the house has fallen ill from fright and grief, and is lying in bed; and my host does not leave her for an instant. Meanwhile I have been able to lay aside a store consisting of 12 lbs of chocolate, some sugar, a few cigars, two bottles of brandy, and some tea, and have packed it all in a small box. I bought the chocolate from a wonderfully pretty girl who, with tears in her eyes, exclaimed to me: "*Ay nostros infelices!* (Woe to us wretches!) What will happen to us when the French come in? Oh how lucky you English are to have your ships and to be able to get away!" This young lady seemed to be very anxious to accompany me, and the temptation was great – but Schaumann was reasonable!'

At 2.00 p. m. Hill's Brigade was embarked, leaving only that of Major-General Beresford still on shore. This brigade was, in effect, the army's final rearguard, and had been detailed to gather together any stragglers, sick, and wounded, still able to be shipped, that the whole might be taken off at a safe point behind the Citadel under cover of darkness. Meanwhile, Corunna's defences were left in the hands of its small Spanish garrison, under the command of the elderly General Alcedo. The 'Soldier of the 71st' approved:

> 'The Spaniards are a courageous people. Women waved their handkerchiefs to us from the rocks, whilst the men manned the batteries against the French to cover our embarkation. Unmindful of themselves, they braved a superior enemy to assist a friend who was unable to afford them further relief, whom they had no prospect of ever seeing again.'

In the event, Alcedo would fend off the French just long enough for the British to depart, before promptly surrendering.[5]

And so, by the evening of the 17th, Hope's whole force – with the exception of Beresford's Brigade – was shipped, and the fleet finally quit port, as Benjamin Miller recorded:

> 'As we drifted down the harbour we saw hundreds of our soldiers, which had been doing duty in the garrison, sitting on the rocks by the water's side at the back of the town, waving their hats and calling for the boats to take them off and as many women and children among them. They saw us pass without seeming to take any notice of them and expecting every minute to be made prisoners, not knowing there were two companies of artillery left on the batteries, which could keep the enemy out of the garrison for that night and indeed not knowing that boats would be sent for them in the night.'

Once safely out to sea, the ships dropped anchor and, as Miller observed, boats were sent back for Beresford's rearguard during the dark hours of night and early morning. General Charles Stewart then concluded his account of the campaign:

> 'Thus, without any other interruption than arose from a feeble cannonade, directed against our shipping, was the whole of the British army, including its sick, its wounded, its artillery, its stores, and even its prisoners, conveyed from the coast; and the first campaign of Britain in the Peninsula closed honourably, though disastrously.'

But it was not quite 'the whole of the British army' – for 100 miles or so to the south, at the port of Vigo, the soldiers of the Light Brigades were awaiting the last of their stragglers and a fair wind, before setting sail for home. They had parted company with the main British force at Foncebadon on 31 December – as will be remembered – in order to ease Moore's supply problems on the Corunna road, protect his southern flank, and secure the port of Vigo as an option for embarkation. Fortunate enough not to be pursued by Soult, these troops had, nevertheless, suffered appalling privations, augmented by the miseries of hunger, cold, and fatigue. Yet they achieved all their objectives, with the loss of fewer than 500 men, thanks largely to their resolute commander, Colonel (later Major-General) Robert Craufurd. 'Black Bob' was a tough Scot, a stern disciplinarian, and a devoted soldier. He was also zealous in the pursuit of duty, freely exercising an infamously sarcastic wit and savage temper. Needless to say, he was feared and respected by his men; yet he kept his corps together, while those of many a more casual commander fell apart on the road to Corunna.

Craufurd's men had made the hills above Vigo on 12 January, when, according to William Surtees:

> 'The view of the town, the shipping, and the sea, broke all at once upon us. It was a most delightful prospect, and it was highly amusing to observe the joy which seemed to animate the woe-worn countenances of our ragged and dirty soldiers. Fellows without a shoe or a stocking, and who before were shuffling along with sore and lacerated feet like so many lame ducks, now made an attempt to dance for joy; laughter and mirth, and the joke now succeeded to the gloomy silence with which they had in general prosecuted their wearisome journey for several days past, as the friendly element before them promised shortly to put a period to long and toilsome wanderings.'

They entered the port just as the ships summoned by Moore were clearing the bay, but happily, 'a sufficient number remained at Vigo to transport us to our native land.'

With no enemy to hinder them, the Light Brigades embarked at a steady, unhurried pace; then proceeded to wait for as long as possible, for those who had fallen behind to catch up. Thus, according to Surtees, it was 21 January before they finally set sail. Perhaps the last man of Moore's army to embark was Private Benjamin Harris of the 95th, who had stumbled towards the shore almost blind with fatigue:

> 'I believe I was the very last of the retreating force to reach the beach, though doubtless many stragglers

were left behind, having come up after the ships had sailed.[6] I managed to gain the seashore, but it was only by the aid of my rifle that I could stand. My eyes were now so dim and heavy that it was with difficulty I made out a boat, which seemed to be the last to put off. Fearful of being left in the lurch half-blind, but unable to call out, I took off my cap and placed it on the muzzle of my rifle as a signal. Luckily, Lieutenant Cox, who was aboard the boat, saw me and ordered the men to return. Making one more effort, I walked into the water. A sailor, stretching his body over the gunwale, seized me as if I had been an infant, and hauled me on board. His words were characteristic of the English sailor: "Hello there, you lazy lubber! Who the hell do you think you are that we should hang around all day for you?"'

Notes

1. According to James Moore, Anderson made a sign to those present, not to mention that Captain Burrard, one of Sir John's *aides-de-camp*, had been wounded in the action.
2. According to Christopher Hibbert, in his book *Corunna*, Lady Hester Stanhope loved Moore, receiving in return the general's sincere affection and friendship, but nothing more.
3. "I surrender."
4. Major Charles Napier was well treated in captivity, and Soult went so far as to send him home to his ageing mother before the formal exchange of prisoners had been agreed.
5. According to Sir Charles Oman, the speedy capitulation of the Spanish garrison of Corunna was due entirely to the machinations of General Alcedo, 'a shifty old man, who almost immediately after took service with King Joseph.'
6. According to George Caldwell and Robert Cooper, in Volume 1 of their work, *Rifle Green in the Peninsula*, some soldiers and their wives arrived at Vigo just in time to see the ships disappear over the horizon. Most eventually made the safety of Portugal; others elected to join the local *guerrilleros*.

Epilogue

The returning redcoats had a rough but rapid ride home, driven by a ferocious south-westerly gale into harbours the length of Britain's southern coast, from Dover to Falmouth, as Sir Charles Oman observed:

> 'Many transports had a dangerous passage, but only two, the *Dispatch* and the *Smallbridge*, came to grief off the Cornish coast and were lost, the former with three officers and fifty-six men of the 7th Hussars, the latter with five officers and 209 men of the King's German Legion.'

The sea-storms persisted for several days after most ships reached home waters, making disembarkation of the increasingly sickly soldiers impossible. When the troops finally did get ashore, between 28 and 31 January – having been cooped up for over ten days in cramped, clammy, unclean conditions – the men looked, as one soldier put it, 'more like the rakings of hell than the fragments of an army!'[1] 'Oh, the filthy state we were all in,' recalled another, 'we were literally covered and almost eaten up with vermin, most of us suffering from ague and dysentery, every man a living, still active skeleton.'[2] Benjamin Harris, who was put ashore at Portsmouth, observed that:

'The inhabitants who flocked down to the beach to watch must have been a good deal surprised at the spectacle we presented. Our beards were long and ragged, and almost all of us were without shoes and stockings. Many had their clothes and accoutrements in fragments, and some had their heads swathed in old rags. Our weapons were covered with rust. Quite a few men, from toil and fatigue, had become quite blind.'

It was the same story at every port the ships put in at. Enthusiastic crowds, eager to welcome the army home, were left sickened and shocked at the sufferings of its survivors.[3] Some harbour officials went so far as to insist that troops be landed at night, so as to spare their townsfolk the harrowing sight of so many returning wraiths. The scale of the disaster was too great, however, to be totally hidden from view, and the British people – accustomed to the pomp and glamour of military parades – were compelled to witness war in its true colours: 'we have the miseries of war brought home to our own doors,' wailed *The Times* on 30 January, 'for the scenes here are beyond any pen to describe.' Meanwhile, according to William Napier, 'the miserable state of Sir John Moore's army became the topic of every letter, and the theme for every country newspaper along the coast.'

Nowhere was public concern more pronounced than at the military havens of Plymouth and Portsmouth. The 'Soldier of the 71st' touched English soil at the former place, noting that:

'Upon our landing, the people came round us, showing all manner of kindness, carrying the lame and leading the blind. We were received into every house as if we had been their own relations. How proud did I feel to belong to such a people!'

Indeed, the whole town rallied to the assistance of the survivors; private coaches were hired to carry the sick and wounded to hospital, and when the wards were full, local families welcomed the remaining invalids into their own homes. Meanwhile, money and clothing were collected for over 900 destitute women[4] and children, who, having endured the retreat, found themselves cast ashore penniless, with no idea of their husbands' or fathers' whereabouts.

The 'Private of the 42nd' also landed at Plymouth, and later penned this heartfelt tribute to its citizens:

> 'Receive, O people of Plymouth, this tribute of gratitude from one of the wretched beings your generous bounty saved from perishing: you made a subscription for us; you gave the poor destitute widows that had survived, and the poor fatherless children, flannel and clothes, and comforts; you covered the naked and fed the hungry ... the blessing of him that was ready to perish be multiplied to you.'

At Portsmouth, a similar state of affairs existed, but with the added complication that the Army's Medical Board – in its wisdom – had seen fit to close the town's main military hospital, in an effort to save cash.[5] Consequently, the crisis was felt more severely here, and James McGrigor, Deputy Inspector of Hospitals for Portsmouth, was obliged to borrow medical facilities from the Navy, while setting up temporary hospitals in barrack-rooms and on board prison ships. These makeshift sickbays were largely staffed by civilian doctors and medical students, with help drafted in from the local militia. Just to make matters worse, however, the number of soldiers listed as sick was growing daily; for if the British Army had gone to war in the thrall of a metaphorical 'Spanish fever', it returned in the grip of a very real one, and according to McGrigor:

> 'Never was situation more favourable for the propagation of contagion than the mode of return of the British army from Corunna. The men were huddled on board with little attention to order. Men of different corps were mixed together in men-of-war or transports, and in the latter particularly, they were exceedingly crowded. The sick and the healthy being mixed together indiscriminately, it was no matter of wonder that the number of cases of fever landed in the last stage of typhus was great; in fact, it was enormous,

and it excited great alarm at Portsmouth and in the neighbouring country when an account of the mortality rate came to be noised abroad.'[6]

It would seem that as many as 20 per cent of the returning force required treatment for typhus and dysentery, though the nature of the remedies on offer varied considerably from doctor to doctor: some recommended hot baths; others, cold; some prescribed spongeing with vinegar; others, bleeding; and some suggested the oral administration of tree bark in wine, or lead, or even cobwebs. In spite of this *pot pourri* of palliatives, 17 per cent of all cases admitted died, though not before infecting many of those sent to care for them, several of whom also failed to recover.

Once the initial shock of the army's expulsion from Spain had sunk into the British psyche, the inevitable crop of questions occurred. How had things gone so badly awry? Why were the soldiers in such an appalling condition? And, more importantly, who was to blame? The British were no strangers to botched expeditions, but the magnitude of the soldiers' sufferings aroused their indignation, and caused them to look for a scapegoat; Sir John Moore, despite his hero's death, was the obvious candidate. According to Arthur Bryant, in his book *Years of Victory*, 'Moore's death saved him from official censure, but many laid the sufferings of the troops at his door, blaming alternatively his inactivity and his precipitate retreat.' So much so, that Robert Blakeney was dismayed to observe that:

> 'A general outcry was got up against Sir John Moore. He was accused of being stupid, of being irresolute, of running away, and of God knows what. His memory was assailed alike by those politically opposed to his party, and by those who once were his supporters, and who, aware of his masculine genius, maintained their posts by basely resorting to calumny and deceit.'

This last was a reference, no doubt, to Foreign Secretary Canning and Secretary for War Castlereagh, who, according to Roger Day – Moore's most recent biographer – deliberately destroyed or suppressed all documents relating to the campaign which cast the government in a bad light. Indeed, the initial reluctance of ministers to defend Moore merely added weight to the words of those who, unpossessed of the full facts of the case, saw every reason to attack him. These even included veterans of the campaign, like General Charles Stewart (Castlereagh's half-brother), who declared: 'The truth is, that Sir John Moore, with many of the qualities requisite to constitute a general, was deficient in that upon which success in war must demand. He wanted confidence in himself'; or the embittered Captain Gordon who, after the privations he had suffered, and the harrowing scenes he had witnessed, was moved to write: 'I am fully persuaded that the distresses the army encountered are chiefly to be attributed to the misconduct of its leader.' As for Sir Richard Hussey Vivian, commander of the 7th Hussars, he could not even wait to touch English soil before censuring Sir John, penning a lengthy criticism of his conduct while, 'on board the *Barfleur*, returning home from Corunna.'

It was not long, however, before the politicos of the Whig party saw, in the deceased general's defence, a sizeable stick with which to beat the Tory government. Thus, Moore's reputation became a political football, pitched to and fro in a game of parliamentary point-scoring. Eventually, however, Sir John's actions were vindicated in the House of Lords, and the first step taken towards rehabilitation. The process was expedited by the efforts of the late general's own family and friends. In fact, Moore's body was hardly cold in its grave, when his brother James published *A Narrative of the Campaign of the British Army in Spain*, dedicated to their grieving mother, and consisting largely of official papers and original letters. Needless to say, the book was an unashamed panegyric, but nevertheless presented a convincing portrait of a man who, though possessed of 'the ancient Roman spirit', was ultimately 'misled by persons who ought to have instructed him'.

Moore's greatest apologist, however, was William Napier, youngest brother to Sir John's *aide-de-camp*, George, and Corunna hero, Charles. Napier's epic *History of the War in the*

Peninsula, published in six volumes between 1826 and 1840, is the bedrock upon which countless histories of the conflict are based; yet he embarked upon this project for the sole purpose of clearing Sir John Moore's name:

> '...a just and faithful servant of his country. The honest loved him, the dishonest feared him. For while he lived he did not shun, but scorned and spurned the base, and with characteristic propriety they spurned him when he was dead ... If glory be a distinction, for such a man death is not a leveller!'

And so, as the facts surrounding Sir John's campaign were brought to light by his supporters, public sentiment changed, and the fallen general was cast in the role of tragic hero. In due course, impressive monuments to Moore graced St Paul's Cathedral in London, and George Square in his native Glasgow, while a flood of elegaic poems was composed in his honour, the most famous being that of an Irish curate, Thomas Wolfe, who was pleased to see his work appear in the local newspaper. Entitled *The Burial of Sir John Moore After Corunna*, and published in 1817, it has since become a classic of English literature, and is, perhaps, Moore's most lasting tribute, ending as it does, in the famous lines:

> Slowly and sadly we laid him down,
> From the field of his fame fresh and gory;
> We carved not a line, and we raised not a stone,
> But we left him alone with his glory!

Indeed, the British Government of the day did not 'raise a stone' – much less carve a line – over the body of their fallen hero. This honour went to Marshal Soult, who ordered the spot where Sir John fell to be marked with a plinth. He also planned a monument for Moore, but was denied the opportunity of realising this noble ambition by a savage popular uprising in Galicia, which forced the French out of Corunna and back over the Cantabrian Mountains. The incoming General Romana, however, had Sir John's remains moved to a more conspicuous location, overlooking the Bay of

Biscay, and over the years, subsequent local benefactors have provided Moore with a tomb, several commemorative plaques, and a formal garden of remembrance. All this for the man who was so desperate to 'beat the French', yet who considered himself, 'abandoned by all things Spanish'.

The postscript to the Corunna Campaign is easily told. As previously stated, the Spanish garrison at Corunna surrendered on 18 January, and the French marched in. Soult treated the townsfolk well, honoured Moore, and arranged for Charles Napier to be sent home to his ageing mother as soon as healing wounds would permit. Nevertheless, as Arthur Bryant points out, 'No sooner had Soult's army, followed by Ney's, overrun Galicia, than that province – hitherto indifferent to the war – rose in passionate revolt.'[7] Weakened by the headlong pursuit of the British, the French armies were thus sent back over the Cantabrian Mountains by a band of belligerent *guerrilleros*.

The mood in Britain was equally bellicose and, while prisoner-of-war General Lefebvre-Desnouëttes embraced the life of a local celebrity at Cheltenham, the country was determined to get back in the ring with Bonaparte as soon as possible. Although Moore had declared Portugal to be indefensible in the face of sustained French aggression, Sir Arthur Wellesley – exonerated for his unwilling part in the Cintra fiasco – had come up with a workable plan for the country's defence at a minimum cost in men and resources. Castlereagh, being a friend and supporter of Sir Arthur's, took his memorandum to the King, and by April 1809 some 40,000 British troops were back in the Peninsula. Five years later, Wellesley – now the 1st Duke of Wellington – had not only secured Portugal, he had also helped the Spaniards cast off the French yoke and, having crossed the Pyrenees into France itself, brought the Peninsular War to a successful conclusion at the Battle of Toulouse. The Spanish heir, Prince Ferdinand, was duly freed from exile and returned to his throne, whereupon he promptly revoked all the liberal reforms introduced by Joseph Bonaparte. Sadly, after eight years of blood shed in his name, Ferdinand proved himself to be a tyrant, becoming hugely unpopular, and provoking a revolt which, ironically, could only be quelled with French assistance.

Meanwhile, Moore's reputation has come largely to rest on the fact that, at a moment when all seemed lost, he staked everything to buy time for Spanish resistance. That he was ultimately obliged to retreat in the face of overwhelming force is beside the point. As Jac Weller points out:

> 'Moore's advance on Napoleon's communications saved the southern half of Spain from French domination for several months. Had Moore not done so, British prestige in Spain would have suffered irreparably.'[8]

Charles Esdaile, in his recent book *The Peninsular War*, refers to Moore's expedition as a heroic defeat, concluding, however, that, 'heroic defeats do not win wars.'[9] Nevertheless, the words of two great generals apparently give the lie to this sound reasoning. Napoleon, musing on defeat in the Peninsula, is recorded as saying, 'It was only Moore's action which stopped me taking Spain and Portugal . . . I admire him for it.'[10] While Wellington, reflecting on victory, humbly acknowledged Moore's part, claiming that, 'We'd not have won without him.'[11]

As for the soldiers who returned from the march of death, what befell them after their deadly ordeal? For most, the answer was simple: another one. For, after a few months' rest and recuperation, much of the British Army was sent on yet another bungled expedition, this time to the Dutch island of Walcheren, in order to seize the North Sea port of Flushing. Once again, supply problems baffled the British, and Lord Chatham, the expedition's chief, was obliged to return home in disgrace, having lost 106 men killed in action, and 4,000 dead of malaria. Nevertheless, many Corunna veterans survived the debacle and managed to see out the whole war, including the bloodbath at Waterloo. It is their diaries, journals, letters, and memoirs, which have formed the body of this book.

It is fitting, therefore, to give the final say to such a soldier, one whose words best sum up the stoical attitude of the average redcoat to the hardships he was obliged to endure. Benjamin Miller, the artilleryman whose pan of potatoes was the first casualty at the Battle of Corunna, thankfully returned home from Spain in one piece, landing at Ramsgate pier with empty pockets and an empty belly. He and his comrades had marched almost 250 miles in eighteen days, from Sahagun to Corunna, over snow-capped mountains, in the depths of winter, chased by a French army bent on their destruction. At the end of this journey, they had turned at bay and defeated their enemy, before sailing home in a hurricane. Now Miller was safe, standing on an English street, gawping at great stacks of food, displayed in shop windows:

> 'But the sight was my share of all I saw, for I had no money and had sixteen miles to march before I could get any, or anything to eat or drink, and a very bad march we had, for it rained the greatest part of the road. But we were well used to such fare, and knew it would soon be over, so we thought nothing of it...'

Notes

1. Harris, Benjamin, *Recollections of Rifleman Harris*.
2. Smith, Henry George Wakelyn, *Autobiography of Lieutenant-General Sir Harry Smith*.
3. One particularly appalled onlooker was the engineer and inventor, Sir Marc Isambard Brunel. Curious to know the primary cause of the soldiers' suffering, he was told that it was shoddy footwear, and was even presented with a sample to take home. He discovered that the shoes contained a layer of clay between the inner and outer soles, which, when damp, disintegrated, causing the shoes to fall apart. At a period when left and right shoes were still unknown, and all footwear was handmade, Brunel set about inventing a machine to mass-produce sturdy, good quality shoes, and proceeded to sell them to the British Army – but not until 1812.
4. Over 100 of these wandering women were pregnant.
5. Army cut-backs were also responsible for the closure of hospitals at Gosport and Deal.

6. McGrigor, James, *Autobiography and Services of Sir James McGrigor.*
7. Bryant, Arthur, *Years of Victory, 1802–1812.*
8. Weller, Jac, *Wellington in the Peninsula.*
9. Esdaile, Charles, *The Peninsular War.*
10. A statement made by Napoleon in exile, and quoted in Appendix II of Napier, William, *History of the War in the Peninsula.*
11. A comment made to his secretary, Fitzroy Somerset, and quoted in Parkinson, Roger, *Moore of Corunna.*

APPENDIX I

Sir John Moore's Order of Battle

Commander of the Forces   *Lt-Gen Sir John Moore*

Cavalry   *Lt-Gen Lord Henry Paget*

Slade's Brigade
   10th (Prince of Wales' Own) Light Dragoons (Hussars)
   15th (King's) Light Dragoons (Hussars)
Stewart's Brigade
   7th (Queen's Own) Light Dragoons (Hussars)
   18th (King's) Light Dragoons (Hussars)
   3rd Light Dragoons (Hussars), King's German Legion
Artillery
   Dowman's Troop, RHA; Evelagh's Troop, RHA

1st Division   *Lt-Gen Sir David Baird*

Warde's Brigade
   1/1st Foot Guards
   2/1st Foot Guards
Bentinck's Brigade
   1/4th (King's Own) Foot
   1/42nd (Royal Highland) Foot (Black Watch)
   1/50th (West Kent) Foot
Manningham's Brigade
   3/1st (Royal Scots) Foot
   1/26th (Cameronian) Foot
   2/81st Foot
Artillery
   Bean's Company, RA

2nd Division   *Lt-Gen Sir John Hope*
Leith's Brigade
  51st (2nd Yorkshire West Riding) Foot
  2/59th (2nd Nottinghamshire) Foot
  2/76th (Hindoostan) Foot
Hill's Brigade
  2nd (Queen's Royal) Foot
  1/5th (Northumberland) Foot
  2/14th (Bedfordshire) Foot
  1/32nd (Cornwall) Foot
Catlin Crawfurd's Brigade
  1/36th (Hertfordshire) Foot
  1/71st (Glasgow Highland) Foot
  1/92nd (Highland) Foot (Gordon Highlanders)
Artillery
  Drummond's Company, RA

3rd Division   *Lt-Gen Alexander Mackenzie Fraser*
Beresford's Brigade
  1/6th (1st Warwickshire) Foot
  1/9th (East Norfolk) Foot
  2/23rd (Royal Welch Fusiliers) Foot
  2/43rd (Monmouthshire Light Infantry) Foot
Fane's Brigade
  1/38th (1st Staffordshire) Foot
  1/79th (Cameron Highlanders) Foot
  1/82nd (Prince of Wales' Volunteers) Foot
Artillery:
  Wilmot's Company, RA

4th (Reserve) Division   *Maj-Gen Sir Edward Paget*
Anstruther's Brigade
  20th (East Devonshire) Foot
  1/52nd (Oxfordshire Light Infantry) Foot
  1/95th (Rifle Corps) Foot
Disney's Brigade
  1/28th (North Gloucestershire) Foot
  1/91st (Argyllshire Highlanders) Foot
Artillery
  Carthew's Company, RA

1st Flank (Light) Brigade   *Colonel Robert Craufurd*
  1/43rd (Monmouthshire Light Infantry) Foot
  2/52nd (Oxfordshire Light Infantry) Foot
  2/95th (Rifle Corps) Foot

2nd Flank (Light) Brigade   *Brig-Gen Karl Alten*
1st Light Battalion, King's German Legion
2nd Light Battalion, King's German Legion

Artillery Reserve   *Lt-Col John Harding*
66 guns
of which 36 were attached to the divisions

APPENDIX II

Sir John Moore's Losses

Figures taken from Oman, *A History of the Peninsular War* and based on the regiments' disembarkation returns for January 1809.

Cavalry

7th Hussars	97[1]
10th Hussars	24
15th Hussars	24
18th Hussars	77
3rd KGL Hussars	56
Total	*278*

1st Division

1/1st Foot Guards	74
2/1st Foot Guards	66
1/4th Foot	149
1/42nd Foot	161
1/50th Foot	264
3/1st Foot	216
1/26th Foot	208
2/81st Foot	241
Total	*1,379*

2nd Division

51st Foot	107
2/59th Foot	143
2/76th Foot	170
2nd Foot	205
1/5th Foot	239

2/14th Foot	138
1/32nd Foot	187
1/36th Foot	243
1/71st Foot	138
1/92nd Foot	129
Total	*1,699*

3rd Division

1/6th Foot	391
1/9th Foot	373
2/23rd Foot	172
2/43rd Foot	230
1/38th Foot	143
1/79th Foot	155
1/82nd Foot	228
Total	*1,692*

4th (Reserve) Division

20th Foot	113
1/52nd Foot	143
1/95th Foot	157
1/28th Foot	302
1/91st Foot	212
Total	*927*

1st Flank (Light) Brigade

1/43rd Foot	85
2/52nd Foot	161
2/95th Foot	96
Total	*342*

2nd Flank (Light) Brigade

1st Light Battalion, KGL	163[2]
2nd Light Battalion, KGL	262[3]
Total	*425*
Artillery and Waggon Train	255[4]
Staff Corps	38
Grand Total	***7,035***

1. Includes 56 men drowned on voyage home.
2. Includes 22 men drowned on voyage home.
3. Includes 187 men drowned on voyage home.
4. Includes 22 men drowned on voyage home, and 9 drowned in Corunna harbour.

Biographical Notes on Major Sources

Robert Blakeney

Born in 1789 in Galway, Ireland, Blakeney entered the army in July 1804, receiving an ensigncy in the 28th (North Gloucestershire) Foot. The gazette which announced this commission referred to him as a 'gentleman' – even though he was still a boy of fifteen. During the Corunna Campaign, Blakeney served in the 1st Battalion of the 28th, this unit forming part of Disney's Brigade within Edward Paget's Reserve Division. After the departure of the Flank Brigades for Vigo on 1 January 1809, the Reserve formed Moore's rearguard and the 28th was continually employed in skirmishing with the enemy and fought well at Corunna. Blakeney's battalion then embarked for Britain, having lost a total of 302 men on the campaign. Within three months of his return from Spain, Blakeney was sent on yet another disastrous mission, this time to the fever-ridden swamps of North Holland. The expedition to the Dutch island of Walcheren in August–September 1809, was an attempt to cause mischief on Napoleon's doorstep. Lord Chatham took the port of Flushing but failed to exploit his success. As on the Corunna Campaign, supply problems ensued and the men picked up a form of malaria which they dubbed 'Walcheren fever'. Chatham eventually sailed home, having lost 106 men killed in battle and over 4,000 through sickness. Blakeney returned too, but was sent back to the Peninsula in January 1810 and remained there till the last shot of that savage war was fired. Having by now reached the rank of captain, Blakeney retired to the Greek island of Zante, where, determined to tell a 'plain and unvarnished tale', he compiled his military memoirs. He died in 1858.

Alexander Gordon

Born in 1781, Gordon was appointed cornet in the 15th Light Dragoons on 9 July 1803, becoming a lieutenant on 22 January 1805. He obtained a captaincy in the 3rd West India Regiment on 18 February 1808, transferring back to the 15th Light Dragoons (Hussars) on 3 March of the same year. During the Corunna Campaign, Gordon's regiment was brigaded with the 10th Hussars, under the overall command of Sir John Slade. Gordon embarked at Corunna with the remainder of his regiment on the afternoon of 15 January, landing safely at Stokes Bay on the 24th. Despite losing virtually all their horses on the campaign, the 15th Hussars lost only twenty-four men, evidence of the fortitude, professionalism and discipline of that corps. Upon his return, Gordon set about compiling his campaign journal, which is highly critical of Moore: 'I am fully persuaded that the distresses the army encountered are chiefly to be attributed to the misconduct of its leader.' He transferred to the 60th Foot on 14 March 1811 and retired by the sale of his commission on 17 October 1812. Captain Gordon received the medal and clasp for the 15th Hussars' celebrated victory at Sahagun, and died at Ellon, Aberdeenshire, on 21 March 1873. He is not to be confused with Lieutenant-Colonel Sir Alexander Gordon of the 3rd Foot Guards, Wellington's *aide-de-camp*, who was mortally wounded at Waterloo.

Benjamin Harris

Born in Portsea, Hampshire, and christened in October 1781, Harris' family home was at Stalbridge, north Dorset, where his father was employed as a shepherd. Harris received no schooling, spending his youth as a 'sheepboy', but later took up the trade of cobbler. He enlisted in 1803, having been selected by ballot, along with a number of other men, for a national Army of Reserve, raised by Order of Parliament, in response to the feared French invasion. Being illiterate, Harris was unable to sign his enlistment papers and was obliged to 'make his mark' instead. After receiving a bounty of £11, Harris found himself in Dublin with his new regiment, the 66th Foot. While stationed there, he was struck with the smart, dark green uniforms sported by a recruiting party of the 95th and volunteered on the spot:

> 'This recruiting-party, who were all Irishmen . . . were the most reckless and devil-may-care set of men I ever beheld, before or since. Being joined by a sergeant of the 92nd Highlanders and a Highland piper of the same regiment – a pair of rollicking blades – I thought we would all go mad together.'

Harris' battalion formed part of Craufurd's 1st Flank (or Light) Brigade during Moore's campaign, embarking at Vigo and thus missing the Battle of Corunna. The battalion lost a total of ninety-six men on the campaign. Like so many other Corunna veterans, Harris was sent on the ill-fated expedition to Walcheren in the late summer of 1809, where he contracted malaria. He was discharged from the army on 10 July 1814, his health ruined by eleven years of hard campaigning and repeated bouts of 'Walcheren fever'.

On Napoleon's escape from Elba in February 1815, Harris was once again called to the colours, but his health was so bad that he was unable to answer this call and, as a consequence, forfeited his army pension of sixpence per day. Thus, he returned to his trade as a cobbler, setting up a shop in London. There he was discovered by Henry Curling, an officer of the 52nd on half-pay, to whom Harris dictated his memoirs:

> 'As I sit at work in my shop in Richmond Street, Soho, scenes long passed come back upon my mind as if they

had taken place but yesterday. I remember the appearance of some of the regiments engaged. And I remember too my comrades, long mouldered to dust, once again performing the acts of heroes.'

'Private of the 42nd'

Although we do not know this man's name, we do know that he enlisted on 7 August 1803 at the age of sixteen. He was recruited at The Black Bull Inn, Glasgow, receiving a bounty of £11, most of which was spent on whisky and treating his newfound comrades. On sobering up, the would-be hero came to his senses:

> 'After coming to myself, I recollected what I had done, and began to think of my family and friends. I had rashly and imprudently abandoned them, having in a manner, stolen away from them ...I then abhorred the very name of soldier ...but I was compelled, sullenly, to submit to my fate.'

During the Corunna Campaign, the anonymous 'Private' served in the 1st Battalion, 42nd (Royal Highland) Foot, an element of Bentinck's Brigade within Baird's 1st Division. Having survived the horrors of Moore's retreat, our soldier's battalion took part in the fiasco of the Walcheren expedition, during which it was decimated by malaria: 'Many who had survived the race to Corunna were now gone to their long homes.' The 'Private Soldier' was one of the fortunate few who returned home from Holland unaffected by 'Walcheren fever' and was soon sent back to the Peninsula. The anonymous hero was finally discharged on 31 October 1814, having completed his term of service:

> 'This was good news to me, for I was tired of soldiering, though the prospect before me was not more bright ...120 men were discharged; some with pensions, but most without any reward for their perilous services, and among the latter number was the writer of this Journal.'

August Schaumann

August Ludolph Friedrich Schaumann was born in Hanover on 19 May 1778. The son of an impoverished lawyer, August's early life was unhappily dominated by this strict and overbearing father, who bullied him into joining first the Hanoverian Army, and later the State Postal Service. Dissatisfied with life in Hanover, August travelled to England in 1803, taking a job as a clerk in Newcastle. Four years later, he accepted a friend's invitation to visit Russia, in order to seek his fortune there. Heavy storms *en route*, however, detained him at Gothenburg during Sir John Moore's unhappy sojourn in Sweden; and when the British sailed away, Schaumann went with them, later becoming a war commissary attached to the King's German Legion.

He survived the rigours of Moore's campaign, arriving back in England with nothing but fifty Spanish dollars to his name. After a few weeks spent recuperating in London, however, Schaumann was eager for more military service, and by May 1809 was back in the Peninsula. After many hazards, feats, and escapades, the Hanoverian adventurer emerged safely from the Peninsular War in 1814. Fortunately for posterity, Schaumann had kept a war diary, which he meticulously compiled upon retiring from the service, 'in Hanover in our small house at number 363 Georgen-Platz, in December 1827.'

'Soldier of the 71st'

Known to have the Christian name Thomas, this Edinburgh man, born in 1790, was another memoirist who, like the 'Private of the 42nd', preferred to keep his family name secret (though the editor of the 1996 edition of his journal identifies a certain Thomas Howell as a possible candidate for the authorship). His parents, though impoverished (apparently subsisting on eleven shillings a week), entertained high hopes for him, paying for his education in the hope of his becoming a man of letters. By the age of sixteen, however, Thomas had developed a rebellious streak and broke his mother's heart by running away to join a troupe of actors. Failing his audition on account of stage fright, Thomas could not bring himself to return home in humiliation:

> 'I wandered the whole night. In the morning early, meeting a party of recruits about to embark, I rashly offered to go with them. My offer was accepted and I embarked at Leith with seventeen others, for the Isle of Wight in July 1806.'

He received a bounty of eleven guineas, and keeping four pounds, sent the remaining money to his mother and father. Thomas, however, soon 'began to drink the cup of bitterness,' as he had not bargained for the brutal life of a soldier. His comrades, bemused by his refusal to drink alcohol, gamble, or swear, nicknamed him 'Saucy Tom' and 'The Distressed Methodist'. He served in the 1st Battalion, 71st (Glasgow Highland) Regiment, during the Corunna Campaign, part of Catlin Crawfurd's Brigade within Hope's 2nd Division. This unit fought on Moore's left wing at Corunna and lost a total of 138 men during the campaign as a whole. Thomas survived further campaign horrors in Holland (Walcheren again), Spain, and at Waterloo, returning home to Edinburgh in the winter of 1815. Having plucked up the courage to confront his long-lost parents, he visited their old house to discover that they had 'flitted long ago'; and so entered a tavern to make enquiries:

> 'The landlord knew me. "Tom," said he, "Are you come back safe? Poor fellow! Give me your hand." "Does my mother live?" "Yes, yes, come in and I will send for her, not to let the surprise be too great." Away he went. I could not remain but followed him and, the next minute, I was in the arms of my mother.'

He lived for a time with his married sister but considered himself a burden, as he could not find employment. In despair, he wrote his reminiscences of campaign life, in the hope of securing some kind of income. He disappeared, however, before his book was published, and was last seen labouring among a party of road menders.

Charles Stewart

General Charles William Stewart was born in 1778 into an aristocratic family. His father was the 1st Marquess of Londonderry and Charles would succeed his half-brother, Robert (better known as Viscount Castlereagh, Secretary for War in the Portland Ministry, and one of the leading British statesmen of the era) to the title in 1822. It was under this title, 3rd Marquess of Londonderry, that he is credited with the book, *Story of the Peninsular War*, first published in 1840. Charles served in Ireland and the Netherlands before becoming one of Lord Paget's cavalry brigadiers (commanding the 7th, 18th, and 3rd KGL Hussars) in the Corunna Campaign. He went on to become Wellington's adjutant-general, 1809–13. Although Moore said of Stewart, 'He is a man in whose honour I have the most perfect reliance; he is incapable of stating anything but the truth,' Stewart was, in fact, both a political opponent and critic of Moore. In his *Story of the Peninsular War*, Stewart writes:

> 'The truth is, that Sir John Moore, with many of the qualities requisite to constitute a general, was deficient in that upon which success in war must demand. He wanted confidence in himself – he was afraid of responsibility – he underrated the qualities of his own troops, and greatly overrated those of his adversary.'

William Surtees

Born on 4 August 1781 at the village of Corbridge, in the county of Northumberland, Surtees' family were, in his own words, 'among the middle classes, my father being a tradesman'. William received basic schooling in reading, writing and arithmetic, though by his own admission, spent 'a dissolute youth, which often caused great pain and uneasiness to my good and pious mother.' Surtees goes on to say that, in his village, soldiering was looked upon as a kind of disgrace, yet he enlisted in the Northumberland Militia in 1798, and later volunteered for the regular army, joining the 56th Regiment and then the 95th: 'I always liked the soldier's life, consequently I did not suffer from many of those parts of it which are so unpleasant to those of a contrary disposition.' Surtees embarked for Spain on 10 September 1808, leaving behind a wife pregnant with their first child. He served with the 2nd Battalion, 95th, which, as a part of Craufurd's Light Brigade, split from Moore's main force at the start of the retreat, embarking unmolested at Vigo. He returned to Spain in 1810, was promoted Quartermaster, and saw much service under Wellington. Following the victory at Salamanca in July 1812, Surtees began drinking heavily:

> '...falling in with a number of officers of very dissipated habits, I was led on to indulge in the most vile and abominable of all vices, drunkenness, to an excess almost incredible.'

After a particularly heavy binge on the occasion of his 31st birthday – a bout which almost killed him – Surtees underwent a kind of painful and all-consuming spiritual awakening, becoming what would now be described as a born-again Christian. In 1815 he was sent across the Atlantic to the United States – thereby missing Waterloo – where he witnessed the British defeat at New Orleans. According to the Preface of his book, 'A severe pulmonary affection compelled him to quit his corps in 1826. He retired to Corbridge, his native village ... till the period of his death, 28 May 1830.' In retirement at Corbridge he compiled his military memoirs, *Twenty-Five Years in the Rifle Brigade*, but he did not live to see his words in print.

Select Bibliography

The following list represents the principal sources used in the preparation of this volume, and I would like to acknowledge my debt to their authors, editors and translators.

Anderson, J., *Spanish Campaign of Sir John Moore*, London, 1905.

Anonymous, *Personal Narrative of a Private Soldier, Who Served in the Forty-Second Highlanders, For Twelve Years, During the Late War*, London, 1821.

Anonymous, *Journal of a Soldier of the 71st or Glasgow Regiment, Highland Light Infantry, From 1806 to 1815*, Edinburgh, 1835.

Anglesey, Marquess of, *One Leg: The Life and Letters of Henry William Paget, First Marquess of Anglesey, K.G., 1768–1854*, London, 1961.

Blakeney, Robert, *A Boy in the Peninsular War: The Services, Adventures and Experiences of Robert Blakeney, Subaltern in the 28th Regiment*, London, 1899; reprinted London, 1989.

Blond, Georges, *La Grande Armée*, Paris 1979.

Bryant, Arthur, *Years of Victory, 1802–1812*, London, 1944.

Caldwell, George, and Cooper, Robert, *Rifle Green in the Peninsula*, Vol. I, Leicester, 1998.

Chandler, David, *The Campaigns of Napoleon*, London, 1966.

Chandler, David G., *Dictionary of the Napoleonic Wars*, London, 1979.

Chandler, David G., *On the Napoleonic Wars*, London, 1994.

Costello, Edward, *Adventures of a Soldier*, London, 1841.

Day, Roger, *The Life of Sir John Moore: Not a Drum Was Heard*, Barnsley, 2001.

Dobbs, John, *Recollections of an Old 52nd Man*, London, 1863.

Esdaile, Charles, *The Peninsular War*, London, 2002.

Fletcher, Ian, *Wellington's Regiments*, Staplehurst, 1994.

Gates, David, *The Napoleonic Wars, 1803–1815*, London, 1997.

Gordon, Alexander, *Journal of a Cavalry Officer in the Corunna Campaign*, London, 1913.

Green, William, (edited by S.J. Teague and D.E. Teague), *Where Duty Calls Me*, Sturminster Newton, 1975.

Hamilton, Anthony, *Hamilton's Campaign with Moore and Wellington*, New York, 1847.

Harris, Benjamin, *Recollections of Rifleman Harris*, London, 1848; reprinted London, 1970.

Haythornthwaite, Philip, *Corunna 1809*, London, 2001.

Haythornthwaite, Philip J., *Who Was Who in the Napoleonic Wars*, London, 1998.

Hibbert, Christopher, *Corunna*, London, 1961.

Howard, M.R., 'Aspects of Sir John Moore's Corunna Campaign, 1808–1809', *Journal of the Royal Society of Medicine*, Volume 84, London, 1991.

Johnson, David, *The French Cavalry 1792–1815*, London, 1989.

Londonderry, Marquess of, *Story of the Peninsular War*, London, 1857.

MacCarthy, James, *Recollections of the Storming of the Castle of Badajos; and of the Battle of Corunna*, London, 1836.

McGrigor, James, *Autobiography and Services of Sir James McGrigor*, London, 1861

Maurice, J.F., *The Diary of Sir John Moore*, Vol. II, London, 1904.

Miller, Benjamin, *Adventures of Serjeant Benjamin Miller, During His Service in the 4th Battalion, Royal Artillery, From 1796 to 1815*, Dallington, 1999.

Mollo, John, *The Prince's Dolls: Scandals, Skirmishes and Splendours of the Hussars, 1793–1815*, Barnsley, 1997.

Moore, James Carrick, *Narrative of the Campaign of the British Army in Spain, Commanded by His Excellency, Lieutenant-General Sir John Moore, K.B.*, London, 1809.

Muir, Rory, *Britain And The Defeat of Napoleon, 1807–1815*, London, 1996.

Napier, William, *History of the War in the Peninsula and in the South of France, From the Year 1807 to the Year 1814*, Vol. I, London, 1835.

Napier, William, *The Life and Opinions of General Sir Charles Napier, G.C.B.*, London, 1857.

Neale, Adam, *The Spanish Campaign of 1808*, Edinburgh, 1828.

Oman, Charles, *A History of the Peninsular War*, Vol. I, London, 1902; reprinted London, 1995.

Oman, Charles, *Wellington's Army, 1809–1814*, London, 1913; reprinted London, 1993.

Parkinson, Roger, *Moore of Corunna*, London, 1976.

Public Record Office: *Documents Relating to Sir John Moore*.

Sarrazin, General, *History of the War in Spain and Portugal, from 1807 to 1814*, London, 1815.

Schaumann, August Ludolf Friedrich, *On the Road with Wellington: The Diary of a War Commissary in the Peninsular Campaigns*, London, 1924; reprinted London, 1999.

Smith, Digby, *Greenhill Napoleonic Wars Data Book*, London, 1998.

Smith, Henry George Wakelyn, *Autobiography of Lieutenant-General Sir Harry Smith*, London, 1910.

Surtees, William, *Twenty-five Years in the Rifle Brigade*, London, 1833; reprinted London, 1996.

Thompson, J.M. (editor), *Napoleon Self-Revealed*, London, 1934.

Select Bibliography

Vivian, Claude, *Richard Hussey Vivian, First Baron Vivian: a Memoir*, London, 1897.

Ward, S.G.P., 'Some Fresh Light on the Corunna Campaign', *Journal of the Society For Army Historical Research*, Volume XXVIII, Number 115, London, 1950.

Weller, Jac, *Wellington in the Peninsula*, London, 1967; reprinted London, 1992.

Windrow, Martin, and Embleton, Gerry, *Military Dress of the Peninsular War, 1808–1814*, London, 1974.

Windrow, Martin, and Mason, Francis K., *Concise Dictionary of Military Biography*, London, 1990.

Index

Index